We Need To Talk About Climate: How Citizens' Assemblies Can Help Us Solve The Climate Crisis

Graham Smith

University of Westminster Press
www.uwestminsterpress.co.uk

Published by
University of Westminster Press
115 New Cavendish Street
London W1W 6UW
www.uwestminsterpress.co.uk

First published 2024

Cover design by Nicky Borowiec

Print and digital versions typeset by Siliconchips Services Ltd.

ISBN (Paperback): 978-1-915445-56-8
ISBN (PDF): 978-1-915445-57-5
ISBN (EPUB): 978-1-915445-58-2
ISBN (Mobi): 978-1-915445-59-9
ISBN (Audiobook): 978-1-915445-76-6

DOI: https://doi.org/10.16997/book73

The full text of this book has been peer-reviewed to ensure
high academic standards. For full review policies,
see: https://www.uwestminsterpress.co.uk/site/publish

To read the free, open access version of this book
online, visit https://doi.org/10.16997/book73 or
scan this QR code with your mobile device:

Table of Contents

Table of Illustrations

Figures

Boxes

Acknowledgements

Many of the ideas in this book have emerged from my work leading the Knowledge Network on Climate Assemblies (KNOCA) over the last three years.[1] KNOCA was established by the European Climate Foundation and aims to improve the commissioning, design, implementation, follow up and evaluation of climate assemblies to enhance impact on climate governance. This means that my perspective is very much grounded in this European (and mostly Western European) assembly practice where most have taken place. I also draw on long experience of working as an academic on democratic innovations and as a climate and democracy activist. KNOCA has brought my passions together in an unsual and unexpected way.

I would like to thank Erica Hope, Alina Averchenkova and Lise Deshautel who came up with the idea of KNOCA and trusted in me to make it happen. Their invaluable advice and friendship has been critical to the project. Thanks to my colleagues and friends at Democracy X (formerly the Danish Board of Technology) who have collaborated tirelessly with me, especially Bjørn Bedsted who twisted my arm to take on the role in the first place. A number of people were willing to read and comment on an earlier version of the manuscript in an absurdly short timeframe. Thank you to Charlotte Billingham, Claire Mellier, David Van Reybrouck, Donal Mac Fhearraigh, Eva Rovers, Jamie Kelsey Fry, John Barry, John Boswell, Kathrine Collin Hagan, Morten Friis, Nabila Abbas, Niels-Kristian Holm, Rikki Dean and Teele Pehk for your thoughts and ideas. I am particularly grateful to Alex Lockwood, John Gastil and (as ever) Susan Stephenson who provided particularly detailed commentary on both content and style. And thanks to Philippa Grand and Richard Baggaley at University of Westminster Press for being great editors and Rob Lee at Noble Studios for the excellent visuals.

KNOCA aims to develop its guidance in partnership with its extensive community that includes policy officials, practitioners, civil society activists and academics (over 700 individuals at the last count). It has been a privilege to work alongside such committed people as we have explored different aspects of climate assembly practice together. I have learned a great deal from collaborating closely with public officials and civil society organisations who have trusted us to support them developing plans for the organisation of and advocacy around climate assemblies. I have been in a rare position to learn with and from governments and radical activists – and everyone in between. Thank you to all of you.

This is my version of that collective learning that I am grateful to be able to share. I hope this book does justice to what I've been taught and to the potential of climate assemblies.

—*Graham Smith*, April 2024

Introduction

In October 2019, 150 French citizens came together in Paris. They had been tasked by President Macron to consider how the country could achieve a reduction in greenhouse gas emissions by at least 40 per cent by 2030 in a spirit of social justice. The Citizens' Convention for the Climate looked like broader French society. Men and women, young and old, urban and rural, school leavers and university doctorates. Among them a surgeon, a concierge, a caregiver, a student, a lawyer, and several people with no jobs or a decent home. All walks of life, working together.[1]

Over seven intense, long weekends spread over eight months – at times delayed by strikes and the Covid pandemic – Convention members heard from over a hundred scientific experts and advocates and deliberated in working groups on different aspects of the climate crisis: housing; labour and production; transport; food; and consumption. Figure 0.1 outlines the structure of the Convention. In June 2020, the members produced their final report with 149 proposals for new laws, regulations and refer-endums. The boldest recommendations included constitutional changes to reinforce 'France's responsibility in preserving biodi-versity, the environment and the fight for climate change.' Other proposals targeted particular policies, such as banning internal flights where a train journey of four hours is available; and restric-tions on advertising high carbon consuming products.

President Macron received the Convention's report with great fanfare in the garden of his official residence. The Convention and its proposals became the subject of intense and at times hostile political and public debate with very different takes on the value of the proposals and the deliberative process. Many of the Convention members came together to establish the organisation Les 150 to promote their report and to scrutinise government action. Sev-eral became high profile figures in social and traditional media.

The Convention reconvened seven months after its report had been published to review government action. Less than one in ten of the members were satisfied with the government response to their recommendations. Some Convention members spoke of 'the feeling of waste, of a tremendous energy remaining unused, of betrayal of promises.'[2]

The government claims that 85 per cent of recommendations have been taken up across different laws and policies, with a number, often in modified form, appearing in the 2021 French Climate and Resilience Law. In response, Greenpeace France has argued that the government has not implemented 'the content or the substance' of the measures.[3]

Whatever the direct policy impact, the respected French think tank IDDRI reflects that the recommendations 'break the silence surrounding the contradictions of current policy.' It goes on: 'By

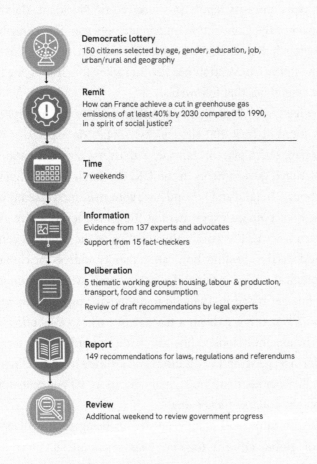

Democratic lottery
150 citizens selected by age, gender, education, job, urban/rural and geography

Remit
How can France achieve a cut in greenhouse gas emissions of at least 40% by 2030 compared to 1990, in a spirit of social justice?

Time
7 weekends

Information
Evidence from 137 experts and advocates
Support from 15 fact-checkers

Deliberation
5 thematic working groups: housing, labour & production, transport, food and consumption
Review of draft recommendations by legal experts

Report
149 recommendations for laws, regulations and referendums

Review
Additional weekend to review government progress

Figure 0.1: The French Citizens' Convention for the Climate © European Climate Foundation.

advancing our understanding of what is possible and acceptable, the Citizens' Convention for the Climate thus presents a new frontier for climate action.'[4]

Four years since its report was received by President Macron, the impact of the Convention on climate policy and its contribution to French democracy remain topics of public dispute. Love it or loathe it, the Convention has become a key touchstone for the climate assemblies that followed.

In the few years since the Convention, activity has multiplied. At last count at least 200 citizens' assemblies on aspects of the climate have taken place in Europe, with over a dozen at national level. National governments in the UK, Scotland, Austria, Spain, Luxembourg, Ireland and beyond have commissioned assemblies.

We've even seen an experiment at the global level, where 100 people from across the world came together as the Global Assembly to address the question 'how can humanity address the climate and ecological crisis in a fair and effective way?'[5] Members ranged from a forester based in Thailand to an Italian yoga teacher who was also a war refugee, from a teacher in Syria to a labourer in India. The assembly looked like the world's population in terms of gender, age, geography, education and attitude towards climate change. Ten per cent had no formal education, 70 per cent were living on ten dollars or less a day.

The organisation and energy needed to bring such a diverse group of global citizens together was phenomenal. Over six sessions between October and December 2021, the members collaborated online to produce the People's Declaration for the Sustainable Future of the Planet. The People's Declaration laid out key principles for how the aims of the UN Paris Agreement could be realised,[6] including a demand to add the right to a clean, healthy and sustainable environment within the Universal Declaration of Human Rights. An interim version of the Declaration was presented at COP26 in November 2021.

We've also seen the setting up of the first permanent assembly In 2023, the Brussels Climate Assembly began its work. It is one of many municipal assemblies that have been organised, but what sets it apart is that it is designed to be a permanent institution. The first cycle of the assembly, lasting four months, brought together 100 residents, reflecting a cross-section of Brussels society, to work on housing, renovation and greening the city. A year later, a new set of Brussels citizens are in place considering food and nutrition, which was, critically, the remit decided by members of the first assembly. And that is how the assembly will continue, each assembly working on an agenda set by the previous one.[7]

The French Convention, the Global Assembly and the Brussels Climate Assembly are examples of citizens' assemblies organised to deal with aspects of the climate and ecological crisis.

But, why on earth would we bring ordinary, everyday people who lack a detailed understanding of the climate and ecological crisis together to consider our collective future? How can that help us? What sets these processes apart from, say, politics as usual, or local self-organised gatherings?

It's this: citizens' assemblies bring together diverse groups of citizens selected by democratic lottery to deliberate on an issue of common concern.

Democratic lottery is the use of random selection to ensure that an assembly is not composed of special interests or only those who are politically confident and articulate, but instead looks and sounds like the wider population.

Deliberation is the careful and considered exchange and inter-rogation of ideas with the aim of coming to collective decisions. It's a long way from the polarised and unproductive interactions that too often characterises our politics.

In a citizens' assembly, randomly-selected people come together to learn, deliberate and craft recommendations on pressing public issues. And no public issue is as pressing as the climate and eco-logical crisis.

The international Organisation for Economic Co-operation and Development (OECD) talks of a 'deliberative wave' of citi-zens' assemblies happening around the world. An estimated 800 deliberative processes have been commissioned by governments at different levels at last count.[8] Given the number that have been held on climate and related issues such as biodiversity loss in the last five years, climate citizens' assemblies – or 'climate assemblies' for short – are at the crest of this deliberative wave.

Support for climate assemblies comes from a variety of sources. Assemblies have been organised by governments of different political hues. António Guterres, Secretary General of the United Nations, described the Global Assembly as, 'a practical way of showing how we can accelerate action through solidarity and peo-ple power'. Perhaps the most voiciferous support has come from activist group Extinction Rebellion (XR), which has protested in London and elsewhere, blocking the streets to demand the setting up of citrizens' assemblies.

Why this sudden interest in climate assemblies? Do they make a difference? Can they help us solve the climate and ecological crisis? Can they help us adapt to a warming world?

These are the questions I aim to answer in this book.

The short answer is that our political systems have failed dis-mally in responding to the climate and ecological crisis. And time is running out – as the Intergovernmental Panel on Climate Change (IPCC) report published in March 2023 states: 'There is a rapidly closing window of opportunity to secure a liveable and sustainable future for all.'

We desperately need new ways to make better decisions, and climate assemblies present one feasible option. An option that is more democratic, inclusive, transparent and effective. What's not to like?

But we have to be honest. The first wave of climate assemblies has not made the difference that many advocates had hoped for. Like the French Convention, almost all climate assemblies have proposed measures that take us well beyond existing government climate policy. Citizens are much braver than their political representatives.

We have only seen partial uptake of their recommendations by governments and in some instances they have been completely ignored – by the political class and the public alike. We should not be surprised. Most assemblies have taken place in the last five years. That's not a lot of time to change a dysfunctional political system. And it's a lot to expect of a relatively new institution.

To effectively address the climate crisis – reducing our greenhouse gas emissions and navigating the perils of a warming world in ways that realise climate and ecological justice – will require a restructuring of our political system. Could citizens' assemblies be a fundamental building block for that redesign? A protype for more inclusive, democratic, participatory and effective forms of climate governance? The answer is yes.

In this book we explore the development of climate assemblies, their impact on climate governance and how that impact can be enhanced and sustained in the future.

Chapter 1 considers the shortcomings of contemporary climate governance and why this has led to growing interest in forms of participatory governance, in particular citizens' assemblies. We set out the core features of citizens' assemblies – democratic lottery and deliberation – and how they can help ameliorate and even overcome some of the failings of climate governance.

Chapter 2 explores how and why the recent wave of climate assemblies was commissioned, revealing the important differences between assemblies. We reflect on the characteristics of the recommendations made by citizens and the extent to which they have had impact. Impact is not just on policy, but also on institutions and climate actors, public discourse and members of assemblies themselves.

Chapter 3 asks how the impact of assemblies commissioned by governments can be enhanced. Four aspects of assembly design are considered: the remit; follow-up by commissioners; stakeholder involvement; and public communication and engagement. Each opens up pathways to impact on climate governance.

Chapter 4 considers future directions for this exciting democratic innovation. Permanent assemblies are being established in municipalities. Civil society organisations are commissioning assemblies to challenge government inaction and enliven public discourse on climate. Systems-thinking can encourage citizens to consider more transformative change. And the diverse, growing movement for climate assemblies has the potential to further embed assemblies with our political systems.

We begin, in Chapter 1, with an examination of the mess we are in – and how we might get out of it together.

CHAPTER I

Why Climate Assemblies?

What if, rather than feeling let down or turned off by politics, we were able to collectively address crises like the climate and ecological breakdown? What if we did not have to worry about political corruption or the misuse of power? What if our fellow citizens were directly involved in the political decisions that affect our lives and those of future generations and the planet? What if we spent time together learning about the challenges we face and deliberating on what should be done? What if our shared wisdom – our common sense – was able to influence what happened? That would sound good, wouldn't it?

The Mess We're In

It's not what we've got, though. Climate governance is in a mess. For more than three decades, scientific report after scientific report has warned that the impacts of climate change will continue to grow ever more severe unless we act decisively, now. The science tells us we need to cut greenhouse emissions drastically. Even then, we need to prepare ourselves for living in a warming world with the flooding, heatwaves and diseases that come in its wake. Our systems, infrastructure and daily lives need to be climate proofed. Economic report after economic report tells us that immediate action will be far more cost effective and, more importantly, save lives. The human, economic and ecological costs can be radically reduced through action in the here and now.

But we do not act. Even at our best, we do not act fast enough.

Why are we in such a mess? Quite simply, these scientific reports have to compete with political and economic dynamics that too often prioritise the short-term and particular interests in our society.[1]

One telling example is the political access and influence of vested interests that profit from the fossil fuel economy and so resist change. Step forward the wealthy and powerful oil companies. Exxon, for instance, knew about the risks of global warming as far back as the 1970s, but chose to spend the intervening decades publicly rebutting the science and funding climate denialists and corporate lobbyists to block action. Even as recently as 2013, its Chief Executive, Rex Tillerson, was willing to state that climate models were 'not competent' and talked of the 'uncertainties' over the impact of burning fossil fuels.[2]

Fossil fuel companies and others who profit from existing political and economic systems have privileged access to the corridors of power and have long been able to shape the story about what progress looks like. Their financial might and capacity to mould our thinking as to what is feasible and desirable reinforces the status quo.

Vested interests aren't just big companies and their lobby groups. The short-term interests of different parts of government can clash with the climate agenda. Departments and agencies are closely tied to these powerful interests. We see this when former ministers take up well-paid jobs in the industries they had until recently been responsible for regulating. Or executives from the fossil fuel industry coming into government as advisors. Remarkably, fossil fuel companies still receive billions in subsidies. We can tell a similar story about the relationship between the meat and dairy industry and government ministries. In the competition for limited governmental resources, climate and ecological action too often loses out. The cross-cutting nature of the challenges we face does not fit within the structures and processes of siloed governments, with most departments and agencies not seeing it as their priority.

Electoral logics create their own challenges. Bearing costs now for long-term benefit is hard to sell across short electoral cycles. Politicians too readily promise immediate gains and fear the electoral backlash against climate action. While the public appetite for action is stronger than politicians assume, it is easier to push the line that the climate and ecological crisis is not so bad. Or a shiny technological solution is round the corner. We just have to sit tight and trust existing political and economic institutions to do the right thing.

This tendency towards political short-termism is reinforced by our political systems granting no voice to those who are going to be most affected by climate and ecological impacts – the young, future generations and those impacted by our decisions in other countries. It is a truism that you need to be present in the corridors of power for your interests to be taken seriously. If you do not have a vote because you are too young or you do not yet exist or you live in another jurisdiction, then your voice is doubly silenced.

Such differences in political power and influence mark our current generations, with particular social groups dominating others. Those from wealthy and privately educated backgrounds monopolise positions of political, economic and social power. These are the very social groups best equipped to navigate the coming storms.

Simply put, electoral politics breaks the democratic promise of political equality for the very people most vulnerable to the dangers of a warming world.

The democratic system seems to be stacked against the long-term decision making needed for climate and ecological action. Scientific evidence has to compete with the dynamics of short electoral cycles and powerful entrenched corporate lobbyists. Those most vulnerable to climate impacts are those most distant from decision making. And these tendencies are further reinforced by growing political polarisation where climate has become a defining feature of culture wars. Alternative facts and conspiracy theories thrive in the filter bubbles created by social media.

This is not a good mix.

If democracy gets in the way, one answer is to give up on it. Cede power to scientists and other experts to make decisions for us. Or an ecological autocrat who will get things done. Lord Martin Rees, the UK's Astronomer Royal, is just one eminent scientist who has made that case: 'Only an enlightened despot could push through the measures needed to navigate the 21st century safely.'[3] But authoritarian regimes have a worse record than democracies when it comes to climate. This apparently simple solution to our collective inertia neglects the evidence that where power is concentrated, power corrupts. The outcomes for the most vulnerable will be worse.

Those of us who are not willing to give up on democracy so fast need to take these arguments seriously. We need to confront them. And we need to offer alternatives. The alternative we're exploring in this book is citizens' assemblies. We're pinning our colours to the mast in the belief that participation of ordinary people in the decisions that will affect their lives and those of future generations and nonhumans can drastically change our politics.

The Participatory Turn

A growing movement is emerging that advocates bringing ordinary, everyday people into the heart of decision making. Even the European Commission – not the most likely advocate for citizen participation – has recognised that 'game-changing policies only work if citizens are fully involved in designing them ... Citizens are and should remain a driving force of the transition.'[4]

So, why this interest in citizen participation in climate governance?

Citizen participation can bring the insights of ordinary people into decision making in a way that increases the robustness of climate policy. It does this because citizens bring their lived experience and knowledge of their local context to the table, shaping policies responsive to that reality. People bring new ways of approaching problems and articulating solutions that are attuned to their interests, needs and attitudes. Social scientists call this the 'wisdom of the crowd'.[5]

Citizen participation can challenge social and climate injustices. If politics is about who gets to be in the room and who defines what needs to be done, then involving citizens can redress existing power imbalances. The politically disenfranchised and those vulnerable to the impacts of climate change can confront policies and practices that privilege those vested interests that profit from the status quo.

Citizen participation can break political deadlocks on climate action. Participation can show that citizens are ahead of politicians on what needs to be done, giving political leaders the confidence and willingness to take action.

Citizen participation can reduce polarisation around climate action. Polarisation is fostered in contexts where people have little or no direct contact with those different from themselves. Those on the extremes fan the flames of fear. Participation can have a very different dynamic. Working alongside those who are different from ourselves can breed mutual respect and understanding.

Citizen participation can increase the legitimacy and public acceptance of social action on climate. As the transition to low-carbon futures unfolds, it will impact people's everyday lives more directly. Knowing that fellow citizens have been part of decision-making processes increases public confidence and builds consent in dealing with change.

Participation can also cultivate a more climate aware and politically confident citizenry. Through participation, we can come to realise that we need to live in very different ways, individually and collectively, if we are going to get out of this mess.

That's the theory at least. Does the promise translate into practice?

The evidence tells us that participatory democracy can work. It has worked. But that does not mean it always works.

Participation can take many forms. It can be open to anyone who is interested, or it can be more targeted. It can give a role to experts or keep them outside the room. It can be organised by public officials or by independent facilitators. It can inform politicians or have power in its own right. A town meeting in the evening for three hours is very different from an online consultation and from a referendum that can change the constitution.

We need to get more fine-grained.

What is a Citizens' Assembly?

The focus of this book is one particular form of participation: citizens' assemblies. And the aim is to better understand when assemblies work, why they work and how we can harness their power for more robust climate governance.

Citizens' assemblies bring together a diverse group of people selected by democratic lottery to learn, deliberate and come to recommendations on pressing public issues. And what is more pressing than the climate and ecological crisis.

Citizens' assemblies have emerged from a broader set of participatory designs that incorporate democratic lottery and deliberation.[6] In other words, the use of random selection to ensure the participation of a diverse group of citizens and a context in which they can learn, share ideas and come to collective decisions. Academics often refer to this exciting family of institutions with the rather dry term 'deliberative mini-publics'.

Back in the late 1970s, two pioneers, Ned Crosby in the United States and Peter Dienel in Germany, independently invented citizens' juries and planning cells respectively. These smaller formats involve around 25 to 30 randomly selected people, although in Germany, planning cells often involve larger numbers when run in parallel or series. The use of citizens' juries has spread, with a number run on aspects of climate change in Australia, Canada and the United States before the recent wave of climate assemblies. The ambitious World Wide Views project linked up a number of citizens' panels on climate and energy across 38 countries in 2009, and then again in 2015 across 76 countries, to feed into international climate negotiations.[7]

In the 1980s, consensus conferences emerged in Denmark, organised by the Danish Board of Technology. Similar to citizens' juries and planning cells, consensus conferences fed citizens' recommendations into parliamentary and policy discussions on highly complex technical and scientific developments that raised serious social and ethical concerns, such as gene technology, the treatment of infertility and surveillance.

A few years later, American political scientist, Jim Fishkin, began experimenting with deliberative polls, a larger format that focuses on the opinion change of a few hundred randomly selected members over a weekend of learning and deliberation. One of his polls, carried out in Texas, provided evidence of informed public support for renewable energy and energy conservation that helped to reshape utility energy provision in the state.[8]

Out of this mix of experimentation, the Canadian provincial government of British Columbia commissioned the first citizens' assembly in 2004. Tasked with designing a new electoral system, this proved to be a game-changer in terms of scale and political empowerment. The 160 members worked over eleven months to come up with a recommendation, which the government then put to a binding referendum. The referendum was lost with the vote falling just shy of the supermajority required. But British Columbia set the bar high for future experimentation.

Most of these deliberative processes happened without much public awareness and relatively limited political impact. This all changed in May 2018, when the Irish voted to liberalise the abortion clause within their constitution. The referendum was called following the recommendation of the Citizens' Assembly 2016–18. The coalition government had decided to set up an assembly because politicians were unable and unwilling to deal with such a controversial and polarising social issue. The way that the Citizens' Assembly was able to review and reflect on the evidence and to produce a collective recommendation on such a controversial issue in an atmosphere of mutual respect set the tone for a change in the constitution and caught the democratic imagination of many beyond the borders of Ireland. As we shall discuss in the next chapter, the same assembly also dealt with climate change, although that was missed by many as the abortion recommendations and subsequent constitutional referendum unsurprisingly caught the headlines.

The Irish Citizens' Assembly set the touch paper alight. It gave licence to those interested in deliberative processes to raise their expectations. And it gave licence to forward thinking politicians and public officials to embrace this democratic innovation. If this was a way to deal with a really tough and socially divisive constitutional issue, how about climate change?

In the next chapter, we'll analyse the development of climate assemblies over the last five years or so. For now, let's dwell a little on why citizens' assemblies are so attractive as a democratic innovation. What is it about democratic lottery and deliberation that is so appealing?

Figure 1.1: The Irish Citizens' Assembly/ICA (An Tionól Saoránach) www.citizensassembly.ie. © ICA.

Figure 1.1: Continued.

Democratic Lottery

Most forms of public engagement attract a skewed group of participants. Think of who turns up to public meetings or participates in online forums. It tends to be politically confident people with strongly held views. Often they are representatives of groups with a material interest in the outcome. Extreme minority positions tend to be vocally articulated, with most people's views poorly represented. Participation lacks diversity and is dominated by those with a strong political interest.

It doesn't have to be like this.

Democratic lottery – often known by the more technical term 'sortition' – stops this happening by using random selection to select assembly members. In this way, assemblies realise the core democratic principle of political equality. Lottery ensures that everyone has the same opportunity to be selected. We use random selection for jury trials in many countries. These have the most profound effects on people's lives. Why not in politics?

This way of realising political equality has at least two attractive characteristics. The first is that lottery ensures a diversity of perspectives are present amongst assembly members. The second is the way in which it contributes to reducing the negative impacts of vested interests and the electoral cycle.

Diversity

Diversity is an unusual quality of most democratic spaces. One of the criticisms of current climate governance is that those making decisions are a long way removed (socially, economically and geographically) from the everyday lives of most people.

Decision makers and the experts they engage tend to come from particular social classes with very similar educational and social experiences. This means a lack of sensitivity to the lives of most of the people they will effect through their decisions.

Recent evidence from the Covid Inquiry in the UK reinforces how the lack of diversity in decision making meant that the interests of vulnerable social groups were not adequately recognised or considered in ways that had profound effects on well-being and livelihoods.[9] Feminists have long argued that the lack of presence of women in decision making means that their interests are not taken into account. We can say the same about those most vulnerable to the impacts of climate change.

Democratic lottery ameliorates the dominance of particular social groups or those with strongly held convictions. Instead, it engenders diversity. Arguably citizens' assemblies are the most diverse political institution we can find in terms of the range of different backgrounds and perspectives in the room. Diversity is both social and cognitive. In other words, members of assemblies bring experiences and knowledge from across society. Social and cultural homogeneity is replaced by heterogeneity.

Equally important is that the wider public can more easily identify with the assembly. It looks like the wider population. We can see ourselves in the process. Survey evidence suggests that this is the case and that identification can generate trust – a scarce commodity in today's politics.

Obstructing Vested Interests

A second virtue of democratic lottery is that it helps protect against the undue influence of powerful vested interests. This takes us back to why the ancient Greeks adopted sortition.[10] In the sixth century BC, the Greek city state was in turmoil. Rich and politically powerful families were constantly at war with one another for supremacy. To cut a long (and very interesting!) story short, selection for positions of public power by lottery in combination with rotation was a way to break that stranglehold. All Greek citizens (then a restrictive category that did not include women, slaves and foreigners) could put themselves forward to be selected by lot to serve on one of the many administrative and legal bodies that kept the system running. The term of service could be from one day to one year depending on the role. Lottery and rotation meant that from one day to the next, you could rule and then be ruled. This had a profound effect on political behaviour and decision making. One class could not rule in its own interest.

By introducing a form of political equality, democratic lottery broke up the divisive and corrupt rule by the rich and facilitated democratic citizenship. It is telling that the philosopher Aristotle defined democracy as sortition, whereas he related elections to oligarchy – the concentration of power into the hands of elites. Yes, elections enable the population to choose between elites, but it is an oligarchical form of political organisation none the less.

Jump a few centuries forward to present day politics and democratic lottery remains a way of breaking up the power of vested interests. Lottery and rotation ensures that powerful groups cannot stack assemblies with their supporters – and makes it so much harder to bribe members, since each assembly is made up of a different group of people and identifying them in advance would be impossible due to the way they are selected.

It is not just the power of vested interests that can be reduced, but also the dysfunctional tendencies of electoral cycles. Members of assemblies are not subject to the same pressures as elected politicians. Assemblies are made up of people who are unencumbered by the electoral calculations that politicians and those who fund election campaigns are forced to consider. Assembly members have the freedom to consider the common good.

Getting Practical

So, how do we get a diverse group of citizens into the room? Unlike jury service, we cannot simply randomly select and legally require people to turn up. Some advocates of assemblies think that is the way to go, but we're far from that point yet.

Most assemblies use a two-stage lottery.[11] Two stage because, first, a large number of invitations are sent out; and second, a diverse assembly is selected from those who put themselves forward.

A bit more detail is needed. Figure 1.2 provides an illustrative overview.

The Invitation

In the first stage, thousands of randomly selected potential recruits are invited. The term citizens' assemblies is a slight misnomer, as the invitation goes to a broader category of people: residents. This is usually by post to randomly selected households, although for the French Convention it was done through randomly generated phone numbers (landlines and mobiles). Letters will often be in an official envelope and on headed paper to increase the chance that respondents take it seriously. The letter explains that the recipient has been chosen by lottery to put themselves forward for a climate assembly, how much time the process will take and

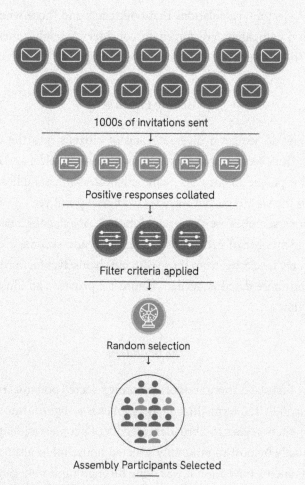

Figure 1.2: How Democratic Lottery Works © European Climate
 Foundation.

the payment they will receive to participate. It will also explain that support can be offered to help with childcare or other caring responsibilities. Those who are interested are asked to return the letter or respond by phone or online giving a few personal details about their background and, occasionally, on their attitudes.

A lot of people will not open the letter at all. Some will read it and think it a scam – why else would they be invited to do such a thing and why would they be offered money? Some won't be interested. Some won't be able to make the dates. But around 5 to 10 per cent will respond. It may be because they are excited about the opportunity to participate in such a process – either out of a sense of civic duty or because they are motivated by the issues being discussed. For others it will be the money or the offer to stay in a nice hotel that seals the deal. For the French Convention, members received €84 per day, the same daily allowance as for jury service, plus specific benefits for childcare and lost income.

Should assembly members be paid? Doesn't this incentivise the wrong reasons to participate? Most advocates and organisers believe it is the right thing to do. Politicians and civil servants are paid to engage in politics. Why not citizens? And does it matter what motivates participation? Isn't it a good thing to have some people in the room who are not so motivated by civic duty or committed to climate action?

Equally important is the provision of care support. How many people who want to participate are unable to because of caring responsibilities? And how many of them are women? If organisers do not offer an honorarium and care support, the pool of volunteers will be full of those with free time and no responsibilities – a lot of retired men and very few single mothers. It would immediately delegitimise the process.

If a diverse group of people is valuable, then it is enhanced if people who would not normally volunteer are included. An honorarium and caring support widen the pool of perspectives and experiences and recognise the service participants are providing.

Organisers have recognised that sending letters to households may not work for all social groups – especially for those who are suspicious of official institutions, often in poorer and minority communities. Extra invitations are often sent to areas of higher deprivation to boost the number of volunteers. We have also seen door-to-door knocking or working through trusted intermediary bodies to raise the number of responses from those social groups more reticent to respond to invitations. The early assemblies in Ireland used market research companies to recruit potential participants through door-to-door or on-street techniques. But not all companies are committed to democratic outcomes. It was no surprise to find neighbours or even relatives appear in the same assemblies as private canvassers took short cuts to recruit people quickly. The Irish have now reverted to sending letters. More recently, the German organisation Es geht LOS has returned to the door-to-door method as a way of directly enthusing potential participants, with impressively high response rates.[12] Some experimentation has also taken place using text messages to increase engagement of young people.

At this point, after the first stage, we will have a pool of a few hundred people who have volunteered to participate. Even with the offer of an honorarium and caring support, it will be a skewed group. It will typically include more people with higher education and income, generally those who are slightly older and less from minority ethnic and poorer communities.

That's why the second stage of the democratic lottery is so important.

Applying Quotas

The final group of assembly members is selected from this pool of volunteers using stratified sampling. Quotas are applied to ensure that assembly members mirror the wider population across salient criteria. That's why volunteers are asked to provide information about themselves. Those stratification criteria vary, but most assemblies include some combination of age, gender, ethnicity, disability, geography, education and social class. Beyond those demographic filter criteria, others may be specific to the remit of the assembly. If the topic is transport, for example, organisers may also include the main modes used by members (public transport, car, bike, walking) or where the person lives (city centre, suburbs, rural) so that salient differences in experience are present within the assembly.

Some climate assemblies have also applied attitudinal criteria. In the UK, recruitment generally includes a measure of level of concern about climate change which can be compared to national statistics. The argument is that you do not want the assembly to be filled with those already sympathetic to more robust climate action. This would mean that not all perspectives are present and critics can quite reasonably charge the assembly with being biased and illegitimate from the start. In some places marked by high levels of political polarisation, such as the United States, voting intentions are also added as a selection criteria to ensure that the assembly straddles political divides. This responds to evidence that suggests that those with a right-wing orientation are often more reluctant to volunteer.

It is the way that the members resemble the wider population that leads some advocates, such as the OECD, to refer to assemblies as *representative* democratic institutions. This is an overt attempt to reclaim the concept of representation from electoral politics. I prefer not to use the term as it tends to confuse. For me, stressing political equality and diversity is key.

Democratic lottery sounds simple, but it is easy to mess up, undermining the legitimacy of the process from the start. Hence the time and resources that most organisers of climate assemblies will spend on this element of the process.

Getting People Through the Door

The two-stage lottery process generates an impressively diverse group that resembles the population across a number of highly salient characteristics. But just selecting citizens and offering them an honorarium is not enough. We need to make sure they get into the room – and then stay. The recruitment process does not end with selection. Democratic lottery must be complemented with effective member support from the start to the end of the assembly. Everything needs to be done to translate the selection of the individual into them walking into the room on the first day of the assembly and then sticking around. Attendance at an assembly can be daunting, practically and emotionally. The organisers will often make sure that transport is arranged along with any care that is needed for family members (including children). But none of the assembly members will ever have been asked to do anything like this before. For some, that will be exciting and increase their motivation to participate. For others, as the start date of the assembly approaches, the more anxiety it generates.

Talking to and building relationships with organisers before the assembly starts can offer reassurance and a friendly, welcoming face. I have heard a number of stories of people who say they would never participate in politics because of mental health issues finding that the support they have been offered means they take that first step. For one person who attended the People's Assembly on Nature in the UK, it was the first time they had left the house since the Covid pandemic. It can be that lifechanging.

For those assemblies that take place online (more common since the pandemic), member support can involve providing wifi and hardware for those without and capacity building for those unfamiliar with the relevant software. Stories have been shared of organisers standing outside a participant's front window during the pandemic making sure that they are comfortable and confident in using new equipment and online platforms.

Most assemblies do an excellent job in translating agreement to participate to people turning up. A lot of time, energy and money are put into the lottery process, the honorarium, caring support and member assistance to ensure a diverse group of citizens come together. And once they are in the room, that support continues and they tend to stay. Confidence in their own and collective abilities blossoms.

Scotland's Climate Assembly is an excellent example. One hundred and five members were selected using a two-stage postal lottery process applying the following criteria: age, gender, household income, ethnicity, geography, rurality, disability, and attitude towards climate change. All residents over sixteen were eligible. The assembly looked like wider Scottish society. Seven replacements were added before the second weekend to cover for no-shows and 102 citizens completed the seventh weekend. That's impressive retention.

Deliberation

If achieving political equality and diversity through democratic lottery is the first ingredient, the second is deliberation. This involves weighing different evidence, ideas and perspectives with the aim of finding common ground and coming to collective decisions. We need deliberation because simply bringing a randomly selected body of citizens together will not in itself generate public wisdom. The danger is that the most eloquent and confident will dominate, and that the group will start splitting into factions and polarising. Diversity plus deliberation is the crucial combination.

Citizens' assemblies facilitate a particular type of interaction. Too much of our political discourse is polarised, with different factions shouting at one another and not listening. Think of how parliaments too often function with politicians aggressively posturing. Or how many social media channels monetise rage, disgust and anger. This is generally unproductive, reinforces more extreme positions and repels people from politics.

Deliberation has a very different dynamic where the emphasis is placed on exchanging and interrogating ideas in a context of mutual respect and mutual learning. The key guiding principle, taken from theories of deliberative democracy, is that decisions are more legitimate when made through a process of free and fair deliberation among equals.[13] This is important for two reasons. First, it is morally right. In a democracy, decisions should not be made based on coercion, deception or misinformation. Political equality must mean more than the right to vote every few years. Second, deliberation is epistemically advantageous. Better decisions emerge when we draw on plural and diverse forms of knowledge, insights and experiences.

Our current politics is too often based on strategic calculations about how 'our side' can win. Instead, deliberation thrives on mutual justification. This pushes us to make arguments in terms of the common good: what is good for society, not our own particular prejudice or interests. In deliberative spaces, arguments based on short-term self-interest get short shrift. In coming to decisions, assembly members weigh evidence, consider those with different perspectives and backgrounds and take a long-term view. Deliberation enhances the capacity of a collective to be fact-regarding, other-regarding and future-regarding.[14]

The psychologist and Nobel Prize winner Daniel Kahneman offers a helpful distinction between fast and slow thinking which gives us a sense of why deliberation is both powerful and challenging.[15] Most of our thinking is fast: fairly automatic and immediate responses to our context without reflection. This is how the brain works most of the time. We go about the world without thinking about what we are doing. Slow thinking enables reflection and is hard work. It requires attention and effort. But we cannot be in that state all the time. We'd never get anything done!

The problem for climate change is that fast thinking comes laden with all those human traits that cause problems. There's optimism bias, which means we underestimate long term challenges. And negativity bias where we place more weight on short-term costs over long-term benefits. Fast thinking is a key driver of short-termism.

In comparison, deliberation activates slow thinking. Citizens' assemblies encourage participants to move away from their automatic and reactive responses that reinforce prejudices, motivating a more reflective and considered form of reasoning and judgement. This is why assembly members get so tired. Slow thinking is hard. Listening and learning together is hard. But this is vital work for democracy to flourish.

So, how is deliberation amongst a diverse body of members enabled in assemblies? How do they generate robust collective judgements on pressing public issues like climate?

Getting Practical

The design of a citizens' assembly is carefully considered to safeguard the integrity of the process. Governance arrangements are put in place to ensure independence and the balanced provision of evidence. The work programme is structured to ensure that assembly members have time and are able to learn, reflect, ask questions and make collective decisions.

The details of how governance and work programmes are structured to promote deliberation vary between assemblies. No single blueprint exists. Much depends on the assembly's remit and the available resources – in particular, time. The more time, the more space for learning, reflection and creativity. But the principles of organisation are the same.

One of the worst criticisms an assembly can receive is that it is biased towards one set of interests within society – that assembly members only heard one side of the story. How can integrity be safeguarded?

Governance bodies for assemblies bring together a variety of stakeholders and subject specialists who oversee the curation of evidence, to ensure balance in what is presented and who presents. As we shall see in the next chapter, governance can be arranged in different ways.

Evidence can take a number of forms. Scientific and policy experts provide insights into the causes and consequences of climate change, existing policy and possible policy options. Advocates offer their analysis and put the case for their favoured solutions. Testimony is often provided by people with direct experience of the consequences of climate change. And aside from these witnesses, the assembly members themselves learn from their fellow members whose varied social positions and experiences mean that they bring different perspectives on climate change into the room.

Assemblies are carefully structured and facilitated to ensure that space is given to members to learn together, to reflect on and scrutinise what they have heard. In the best assemblies, knowledge exchange happens in different ways that respect the different learning styles of members. It is not just an expert at the front of the room going through a series of PowerPoint slides. Not everyone learns through such cognitive and textual approaches. Learning can be more active and sensory, through imagery, movement, serious games and excursions.

Assembly members have time to process what they have learned together, sift the evidence, ask questions, seek clarifications and develop their collective responses. Much of this work is organised in small groups to ensure space for members to contribute and to build mutual respect and collaboration. The work of assemblies is arranged so that it is members who are in control and not the more experienced technical experts or advocates who are providing evidence.

One of my favourite facilitation techniques commonly used in assemblies is the evidence carousel. Witnesses will give a presentation that must be short and accessible. Commonly, the next step would be for presenters to take questions from the front of the room in a format where they are the centre of attention and power dynamics are in their favour. This is usually an unsatisfactory experience for most. Assemblies will often subvert that dynamic. Members work in small groups to reflect on what they have heard and come up with a list of questions and issues they would like to hear more on. At that point, the witnesses spend time at each table, with the members leading the discussion and focusing on their particular areas of interest. The power dynamics shift completely, with the witnesses at the service of the members. 'Experts on tap, not on top' is a common refrain.

As we shall see in the next chapter, the first wave of climate assemblies approached their governance and programme in slightly different ways. For example, the organisation of some assemblies has been led by seconded civil servants, others by independent democracy practitioners. Some assemblies break into workstreams to tackle different dimensions of the remit, others work as a single assembly. Some adopt more directive table facilitation to encourage equality of voice between assembly members, ensuring that that less confident members feel able to contribute and those more confident give space to others to speak. Others prioritise collective agency and creativity, allowing members to self-organise and only intervening if problems in group dynamics emerge.

Whatever the particularities of the design of assemblies, the aim is to create an environment within which the diversity generated by democratic lottery is combined with structured and facilitated deliberation. It is these two characteristics of citizens' assemblies that promise an alternative to the dysfunctionalities in our current politics and can promote a more robust and democratic response to the climate crisis.

CHAPTER 2

Learning From the First Wave

The number of climate assemblies that have been commissioned since the French Citizens' Convention for the Climate began its work in October 1999 is striking: at least 200 taking place across Europe. In the last five years, roughly half of the 'deliberative wave' identified by the OECD has been made up of climate assemblies. Most of these assemblies have been organised at municipal level. A dozen or so have taken place at national level, along with an experiment at the global level. Figure 2.1 gives a sense of the spread of assemblies across Europe, although not all of them have been identified.

It is rare for national governments and agencies to commission citizens' assemblies. Some have been particularly impressive in their size and scale. These national assemblies will be the main focus of this book. This is not to discount the importance of municipal or regional levels, but in general national assemblies have more potential to create systematic shifts in climate governance. Whether they do so is another matter.

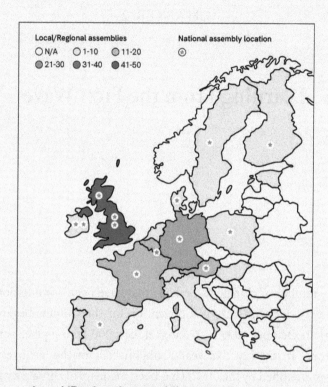

Local/Regional assemblies

UK	50	Italy, Spain, Switzerland	5
Germany	26	Finland, Hungary	3
Netherlands	20	Estonia, Ireland, Portugal	2
France	18	North Macedonia, Sweden	1
Austria	15		
Poland	13	Brazil, Japan, Maldives	3
Belgium	11	Canada, Lebanon, USA	1
Denmark	10		

Figure 2.1: Map of Climate Assemblies across Europe © European Climate Foundation. This map is based on data from KNOCA and is likely to be an underestimate.

The context of their commissioning, remits, structure, resourcing and impacts of these assemblies have varied wildly. Capturing some of these differences is important because they affect the potential futures for climate assemblies and the extent to which they might help reshape climate politics.

While the number of assemblies in recent years is striking given the low level of activity previously, we need to remember that 200 is not that many given the number of public authorities across the world. The OECD has done a great job promoting the deliberative wave, but climate assemblies are still a fairly niche political institution.

One of the challenges in making sense of this area of democratic innovation is the different ways that the terms 'citizens' assembly' and 'climate assembly' have been used. The same term is often used for very different forms of participation. It can all get very confusing. When we use the term 'climate assembly', it is shorthand in two specific ways.

First, climate is shorthand for the broader climate and ecological crisis. We therefore include assemblies that primarily focus on issues such as biodiversity loss as well as other areas such as transport or urban planning, but where climate is a key consideration.

Second, our interest is in the combination of democratic lottery and deliberation and so we include processes that go by the name of citizens' juries and citizens' panels. Where assemblies end and juries start is an unanswerable question because those terms have been used interchangeably. Ours is a broad definition.

The iconic climate assembly is arguably the French Citizens' Convention for the Climate. It is the first time that a dedicated national climate assembly was commissioned on such a large scale. While Ireland's Citizens' Assembly 2016–18 predates the

Convention, climate was only one of the issues it considered and over much less time. Climate Assembly UK began its work a few months after the French Convention started but was a more circumscribed process because it had fewer resources at its disposal. Within a year of the Convention and the UK assembly finishing their work, three other national assemblies were underway in Scotland, Denmark and Germany, plus a smaller citizens' jury in Finland. In 2022, a further seven national assemblies began their work in Austria, Luxembourg, Poland and Spain with the assemblies that year in Ireland and the UK the first to specifically focus on the nature crisis and biodiversity loss. And in Ireland, the adult assembly was complemented by a children and young people's assembly. Two national-level climate assemblies in the Netherlands and Norway are being planned for later in 2024. The Knowledge Network on Climate Assemblies (KNOCA) provides summaries and links to all of these national assemblies.[1]

This chapter has three ambitions. First, it aims to capture some of the similarities and differences in the commissioning, design and implementation of climate assemblies across Europe.[2] They all share the combination of democratic lottery and deliberation. Beyond that, important differences in practice emerge. We then ask the question of what citizens want. When they have the opportunity to learn, reflect and collaborate, what do they propose? And finally, we ask whether all this time and effort to engage citizens has had any impact. Not just on policy, but also on institutions, public discourse and the members themselves.

The main lessons we learn are that climate assemblies vary considerably in the way they are designed and delivered and that their impacts vary too. But in almost all cases, the recommendations proposed are far more ambitious than existing government policy.

How Climate Assemblies Work

When most people think of citizens' assemblies, they have in mind a process commissioned by government. Government sets the remit. Members selected by democratic lottery come together to learn from experts, advocates and those with direct lived experience. They deliberate and make recommendations. And then the government responds – hopefully implementing many of the proposals or explaining why it is not acting. That's the 'standard operating model' for climate assemblies.[3]

While this is the common basic structure, plenty of variation happens in practice. Variation in political context. Variation in who commissions. Variation in remit. Variation in size and scale. Variation in governance arrangements. Variation in how the work of the assembly is structured and facilitated. Variation in engagement with wider publics. Variation in number of recommendations. Variation in what happens to recommendations (see Box 2.1).

It is a mistake to think that all climate assemblies are the same.

Political Context

In a couple of cases, assemblies have been organised as a direct response to major political crises. The French Convention emerged out of extensive social disruption – most notably the Yellow Vests protests which had mobilised in response to the potentially regressive impact of President Macron's proposals for an increase in the carbon tax, a reduction of speed limits mainly in rural areas and tax cuts that would not benefit the poor. As part of his response to the protests, Macron organised a Grand National Debate that took place in early 2019 across a

Political context	Which social and political factors led to the organisation of an assembly?
Commissioner	Which institution commissioned the assembly?
Size and scale	How many members and how much time?
Democratic lottery	How diverse is the membership?
Remit	What is the assembly's task?
Governance	How is the integrity of the assembly ensured?
Work programme	How is the work of the assembly organised?
Facilitation	How is the relationship between members and with witnesses managed?
Communication and public engagement	How do broader publics engage with the assembly?
Report and recommendations	How does the assembly present its proposals?
Official response	How does the commissioner respond (if at all)?
Monitoring	What oversight is put in place to scrutinise action?

Box 2.1: Key Features of Climate Assemblies.

whole range of policy issues. The Debate included a number of regional deliberative processes. The experience of the Debate sensitised those around the President to the potential of assemblies. More moderate Yellow Vests and ecological and democracy activists who came together under the 'Citizen Vest' banner exploited the policy window, producing a series of demands including a climate assembly. This idea was also championed by Cyril Dion, a high-profile documentary maker. President Macron was looking for a way to respond to public disquiet about climate. A Citizens' Convention for the Climate was an idea whose time had come.

The Irish Citizens' Assembly 2016–18 can be traced to a political crisis of a different sort. The nation suffered greatly during the financial crisis, with significant loss of trust in the political system. Political parties were looking for new forms of governance to help rebuild confidence in the system. An experimental citizens' assembly organised by academics and civic activists as a demonstration project in 2011 captured the attention of key politicians and journalists. A year later, a version of the assembly model – the Convention on the Constitution, one third of which was made up of elected politicians – was established by parliamentary resolution following a commitment by the coalition government. The Citizens' Assembly 2016–18 was promised in the coalition agreement after the next election. A decade on from the government first commissioning a citizens' assembly and they have become part of the institutional furniture, with the Citizens' Assembly on Biodiversity Loss reporting in 2023.

Social movement pressure had some influence on the establishment of other national assemblies, although this was never to the level of street protest in France. Extinction Rebellion (XR), particularly across the UK, linked its disruptive protests with the demand for a citizens' assembly on the climate and ecological emergency. In Austria, the Citizens' Climate Assembly was organised in response to the demand of a citizens' initiative on climate protection (Klimavolksbegehren) which collected 380,000 signatures, well over the required threshold for a parliamentary debate.

Finland, Sweden and Luxembourg are distinct outliers. Both the Finish and Swedish assemblies came out of academic research projects. In Luxembourg, the assembly was a surprise announcement by the Prime Minister.

Commissioners

Who commissions assemblies also differs and can have a profound effect on their connection with, and influence on, policy and the political system more broadly.[4] The French Convention was commissioned by the President of the Republic, thus giving it a high political profile. The Luxembourg Climate Citizens' Council commissioned by the Prime Minister.

In Ireland, governments propose assemblies but their terms of reference are laid down by parliament, which then requires the government to take the lead in commissioning. It is the responsibility of the core executive to deliver. In Scotland, the parliament introduced an assembly within climate legislation, although in this case, it did not have the same degree of support from within the government as enjoyed in Ireland.

In Austria, Denmark and Spain, while the government made a formal commitment, particular ministries led the process. Ensuring whole government buy-in is more difficult in such circumstances.

Climate Assembly UK is an unusual example as it was commissioned by six parliamentary select committees to inform their work scrutinising government policy and action on climate across different policy areas. The UK assembly had no direct relationship with government.

Three of the national assemblies – in Germany, Poland and the People's Assembly for Nature in the UK – are even more unusual. They were commissioned directly by civil society organisations as part of their campaign and advocacy strategies. We will have more to say about the motivations and strategies behind assemblies organised by non-state actors later in the book.

Size and Scale

The main determining factor for the size and scale of assemblies is money. Some commissioners are simply more generous with budgets and other resources such as secondment of staff. Budgets have varied wildly.

The assembly that has outstripped all others is the French Convention with a budget just shy of €7 million. Austria had a budget of around €2 million, with Scotland coming in a little lower. Compare these figures to the Danes with less than €100,000. In this case, the Danish Board of Technology, the organiser of the assembly, was willing to take a hit on the budget as they wanted to make sure it went ahead. We have to be careful about making comparisons, because some costs may be hidden – for example, the salary costs of civil servants working on the project. But this cannot explain the difference in budgets available between countries. The French and the Austrians could afford to bring the assembly together in person over a number of weekends and to dedicate sizeable proportions of their budget to communications. The Danes had to accept less in-person time for members and spent next to nothing on engaging the media.

National assemblies tend to aim for around 100 members. This is a symbolic figure that appears to resonate with policy makers. It has no particular statistical significance. The largest assembly to date was the German Citizens' Assembly on Climate with 160 members, with the French Convention at 150. The outlier is Finland's Citizens' Jury on Climate Action involving only 33 people.

The big difference between assemblies is in the time that members spend together. Figure 2.2 captures this variation. Their budget allowed the French to bring the 150 members to Paris across eight long weekends, including a weekend to review the government response.

The Scottish had a similar structure to the French. They could afford to work on this scale because the assembly took place entirely online during the Covid pandemic – travel and accommodation are some of the biggest items for assembly budgets. Both France and Scotland were able to accommodate an extra weekend at the request of the members. It is common for members to ask for more time, but rare to be able to do this because of scarce resources.

The Austrians and the Spanish were almost at the same scale – 100 citizens working over six weekends. The Spanish also ran their assembly almost entirely online until the final weekend of voting, with most members meeting in person with a few remaining online.

The idea of blended assemblies is catching on, with the four-weekend People's Assembly for Nature explicitly designed with face-to-face weekends at the start and end and its two middle weekends online. For the organisers, the in-person weekend at the start was particularly crucial to develop strong relationships between members and at the end to support collaborative recommendation-writing.

The Danes were the first to run a two-phase process to model how a permanent assembly might work. For the second phase, a third of the first assembly remained with the rest replaced. The limited budget meant that both phases combined two weekends with evening meetings.

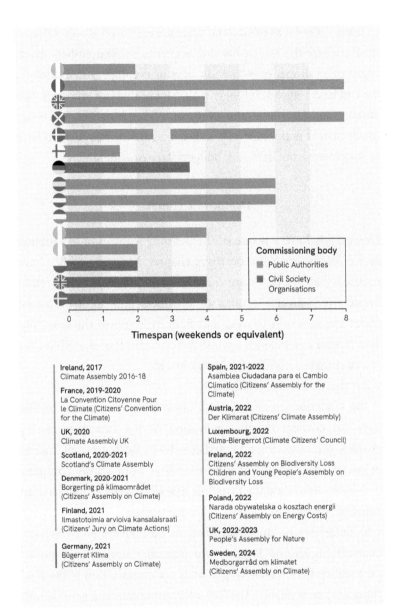

Figure 2.2: Variations in Scale of National Climate Assemblies
© European Climate Foundation.

These differences in size and scale are mirrored at sub-national levels, where the salient number seems to be 50 members meeting over a number of weekends, days or evenings. Again though, we can find bigger and longer processes and many that are much smaller and shorter – and every other combination. Costs are lower than at national level because it is rare for members to have to stay overnight. That said, budgets vary considerably.

Democratic Lottery

Democratic lottery is one of the defining features of assemblies, as we discussed in the previous chapter. Most assemblies have ensured that resources are made available to attract and retain impressively diverse groups of members and are transparent about the selection process and final make-up of the assembly. This is vital as a defence against the criticism that assemblies are full of climate activists and sympathisers.

But this is not always the case.

The Luxembourg and Spanish assemblies are unusual in that they cut corners in the application of the two-stage lottery process, not following accepted standards. Both drew all (Spain) or part (Luxembourg) of their members from survey company panels, undermining the principle that all citizens should have an equal opportunity to be selected to participate.

In Luxembourg, applicants had to be conversant in French, Luxembourgish and English which further undermined political equality. Unfortunately, the details of composition of the final panel are not available. The lack of transparency is a general tendency for this assembly, with no details of the work programme or who gave evidence available on its website.

A couple of assemblies have faced challenges with retention. Out of the 99 members for each phase of the Danish assembly, in the first phase, only 59 voted. In the second phase, 68. This may well relate to the limited resources available to support members during the process compared to better funded processes.

The Luxembourg Climate Citizens' Council also had retention issues, partly because it had to extend its work unexpectedly as we will discuss below. It was scheduled over five weekends, but a less formally organised process took place over the summer to complete and vote on the recommendations. Out of the 100 members that started the process, 63 voted.

Remit

Climate assemblies are not asked to do the same things. Their remits vary. The remit of the first national assembly in Ireland was to recommend actions by the state to make it a leader in tackling climate change. Up to that point, the Irish were seen as laggards in climate policy across Europe. This is a broad remit, particularly given that the assembly worked over only two weekends.

Remits that followed went even broader, not limiting members to considering state action. Many assemblies have focused on climate mitigation and achieving national commitments under the UN Paris Agreement. For example, 'How can France cut greenhouse gas (GHG) emissions by at least 40 per cent by 2030 compared to 1990, in a spirit of social justice?' And in Austria, 'How to reach climate neutrality by 2040?'

In Scotland and Spain, the remits broadened further, creating the space for members to deliberate on adaptation: 'How should Scotland change to tackle the climate emergency in an effective and fair way?' and 'A safer and fairer Spain in the face of climate change. How do we do it?'

The Polish assembly is the outlier, with its distinct task to propose measures to counteract energy poverty.

We find variations in remits for climate assemblies at the local and regional level. The main difference is that many more subnational assemblies have had tighter remits to propose measures on specific policy areas, such as flooding, transport, air pollution, and green areas.

Arguably the broadest remit is that of the Global Assembly that deliberated on the question, 'How can humanity address the climate and ecological crisis in a fair and effective way?'

We will have more to say about the relative merits of different remits in the next chapter.

Governance

How to ensure the integrity of climate assemblies? Critics have been quick to raise questions of their independence. Criticisms take two contrasting forms. Either, the assembly is a form of 'citizen-washing', where the government is using the assembly to legitimise decisions already made. Or the assembly is dominated by climate interests – if the assembly itself is not full of climate activists, those that organise the process are biased in that direction. While they come from different perspectives, both criticisms raise questions about the integrity of the process, specifically the independence and balance of governance arrangements.

Integrity is achieved in large part by ensuring a variety of stakeholders and technical experts are integrated into the governing of the process, along with an independent design and delivery organisation with experience in organising participatory and deliberative processes. What better way of ensuring balance and integrity than by including competing interests in assembly governance? Involving stakeholders has the additional benefit of buy-in to the process and a greater chance that they will take seriously any recommendations that are directed at their activities.

Two governance bodies are typically created, although in some settings, particularly at more local levels, they may be combined into a single body. An advisory stakeholder body is appointed to oversee the design and delivery of the assembly and to ensure it is informed by different social perspectives. Stakeholder groups include the representatives of different social, economic and environmental interests. For example, in Austria, its Stakeholder Advisory Board included representatives from the Chamber of Commerce, agriculture, labour unions, climate and social justice NGOs and youth. The Stewarding Group in Scotland also included members of political parties and experts in deliberative processes.

The evidence group, knowledge committee or scientific board is the second common governance body. It is made up of technical experts from different disciplines, usually from universities and sometimes civil society organisations. It provides advice on the curation of knowledge in the assembly: on what evidence to present and who should do it. The members of the evidence group are often appointed with advice from the stakeholder group. The evidence group in the Global Assembly faced the challenge of integrating scientific and indigenous knowledge holders which created tensions. This is an area where assemblies need to innovate to ensure different epistemic systems are respected.

An organisation with experience in designing and delivering deliberative processes is typically appointed. A small industry of professional participation organisations has emerged across Europe over recent years that provides services to governments and other providers.[5] Many are third sector, not-for-profits. Most are deeply committed to high standards of integrity, but as the demand increases, we can expect to see some less scrupulous players enter the market which may well effect quality.

Their role is to design and then facilitate the assembly. They are often quite small organisations and call on a network of self-employed facilitators. At times, particularly at local level, they may train public administrators or volunteers to play those roles. This can then give the local authority increased skills and capacity to deliver its own deliberative processes. The local council in Kingston in the UK, for example, commissioned a citizens' assembly on air pollution from Involve, an independent participation organisation that has delivered Climate Assembly UK, Scotland's Climate Assembly and the People's Assembly for Nature. The council used the assembly as an opportunity to train its own staff in deliberative practices which meant it could deliver a more cost-effective assembly on regenerating the city centre a few years later.

One of the differences in governance regimes is the extent to which the professional participation organisation takes a leading role in the project. For example, in Austria, the participation practitioners led the co-ordination of the design and delivery of the assembly, working closely in a core team with a public official from the responsible Ministry, two co-ordinators of the Scientific Board and colleagues involved in public communication and engagement. That kind of working arrangement is often replicated in municipal and regional level assemblies.

The Irish developed a slightly different model, that was also adopted by Scotland. The lead body for assemblies in those nations is a secretariat of seconded public officials. It is their role to appoint and co-ordinate the work of the participation organisation, the stakeholder body and the evidence group. The Irish appoint an independent Chair to formally lead the process and act as a figurehead for media and public engagement. This set up was borrowed from the original British Columbia Citizens' Assembly on Electoral Reform. The Chair of the Irish citizens' assembly that dealt with climate was a judge; for the assembly on biodiversity loss, an academic. Scotland appointed two public figures to act as independent Chairs.

The central role of public officials in co-ordinating the process in Ireland and Scotland and in many local processes can lead to questions about the assembly's integrity. It is a difficult balancing act because the assembly can be criticised for a lack of independence and being too vulnerable to government interests. However, the close involvement of public officials can help smooth the process of integrating the assembly and its recommendations into the government's work. After all, they know how the system works and who to contact.

The French Convention took a different approach to governance arrangements, although still embracing the principle of involving diverse interests and climate experts and ensuring oversight. A single Governance Committee was appointed to organise the assembly, with three independent Guarantors with high public profiles to ensure the independence and deliberative quality of the process. The members of the Committee comprised major social interests, including representatives of the economic, social and environmental sectors, climate experts, participatory democracy experts and appointees of the Ministry.[6] In other words, the French rolled into one body the functions of the stakeholder and evidence groups along with participation expertise. But the Committee was not an advisory body. Rather it had executive powers to design the Convention process. It did employ three professional participation organisations, but their role was more limited compared to other assemblies, and very much subservient to the Governance Committee. Once the assembly began its work, the Governance Committee established an evidence group to help it access relevant experts and advocates to deliver the Convention's programme of work.

The Committee found its executive work of designing the assembly hard to achieve at times because of the number of voices at the table. Too many cooks spoil the (deliberative) broth? Many of the Committee members had little or no direct experience with citizen participation. Some had quite conservative attitudes about the capacities of citizens to deal with complex issues and were minded to constrain the Convention's agenda and activities.

An important mediating factor turned out to be Convention members. Once the Convention began its work, two randomly selected members joined the Governance Committee. They rotated after each Convention weekend. The assembly members were able to break some of the deadlocks within the Committee, challenging those who had less faith in their capacities. The agenda of the Convention was less tightly managed as time progressed. The inclusion of assembly members in governance bodies has happened elsewhere, for example in Denmark, where the practice transferred from earlier experience with consensus conferences.

Where most assemblies carefully consider governance arrangements, Luxembourg again stands out in the way that governance was an afterthought. An advisory group was not put in place until after the second weekend so was not able to oversee the early design work. Partly this is because of how quickly the assembly was commissioned; partly it was down to a lack of experience amongst the organisers. When it was established, the advisory group was made up of mostly participation and deliberation experts. No stakeholder or evidence group was created.

A final element of governance arrangements that is receiving more attention is arbitration. What happens if significant disagreements and conflict emerges within or between elements of the governance arrangements? Many assemblies do not codify the responsibilities of different bodies. Even with codification, Marcin Gerwin, a pioneer of climate assemblies in Poland, has made a compelling case for appointing independent arbitrators – in his case, arguing that this role should be taken by respected academics who are not directly involved in the assembly process.[7] With so many interests in play, this is an important innovation in practice.

Work Programme

How do we ensure that members are able to fulfil the remits they have been set? A common feature is that evidence is generally presented in plenary sessions, while reflections on learning and other collaborative work happens in smaller groups. These processes are facilitated to promote deliberation.

One difference between assemblies is that some have taken place partly or fully online. The platforms that organisers have chosen to use – typically Zoom or similar – have functionality that allows close replication of in-person design, including smaller break out groups for more intimate deliberation and collaborative working. What digital platforms cannot do, however, is fully replicate the informal spaces such as coffee and lunch breaks that play an important role in developing trust and cohesion across an assembly.

Given the broad nature of most remits, it is common practice for the whole assembly to spend time learning about the climate and ecological crisis and the current context of climate policy and then to split into workstreams in order to cover as much ground as possible. The French and UK assemblies were the first to do this. In France, the members of the Convention were randomly assigned to five thematic groups defined by the Governance Committee: housing; labour and production; transport; food; and consumption. Climate Assembly UK divided into three workstreams: how we travel; in the home; what we buy, land use, food and farming. Many of the other assemblies followed the same pattern. Denmark differs in that rather than the organisers defining the workstreams, it was left to members to decide which areas to prioritise – again a practice drawn from their experience with consensus conferences. Workstreams hear from witnesses specific to their policy area and then break into smaller groups for collaborative work.

Most assemblies have been tasked with generating their own recommendations. Climate Assembly UK and the Finnish Citizens' Jury are the exceptions to date. Each of the UK assembly's workstreams focused on evaluating three alternative scenarios and sets of policies. During the last session, the assembly worked as a whole on generating its own recommendations on electricity production, greenhouse gas removal and the impact of Covid-19. The Finnish Jury focused solely on evaluating the fairness and impact of 14 potentially controversial measures that the government was considering for its medium-term Climate Change Policy Plan – focusing on policy evaluation rather than policy development.

One of the challenges faced by organisers is how to ensure that the groups within and across different workstreams understand what others are doing and to ensure that proposals do not conflict with each other. Within workstreams, different groups will often share their draft proposals with other groups in order to get feedback, or in some instances will rotate who is working on particular proposals. Assemblies have tried different approaches to develop learning and feedback across workstreams, such as marketplaces where different groups present their work. Some have made use of online platforms to enable comments and suggestions.

Assemblies have also developed strategies to work on issues that cut across all policy areas, with more or less success. The French tried to establish what they termed a 'transversal' workstream on finance and governance. It only lasted for two sessions and was suspended when some members complained that it seemed to be taking a more important role than those working on the individual themes. In Austria, two transversal themes were identified – global responsibility and social justice – which were considered by all workstreams and were the specific focus of one of the weekends.

A smaller number of national assemblies have not broken into workstreams, but rather stayed together to work through the issues as a single body. In Ireland this is the approach taken by all its national assemblies. Assemblies cannot get through as much work, but recommendations have been considered to the same depth by all members.

The Luxembourg assembly was designed with the intention that the whole assembly would work together to produce recommendations, following the Irish approach. The organisers misjudged the work programme, not giving enough time for members to deliberate and develop robust recommendations. After the original five in-person weekends that had been tightly facilitated around different topics, the government agreed to extend the time available, but did not provide further budget. The organisers had to opt for a more self-organised process with six working groups led by 15 spokespeople elected by assembly members. These groups further developed the recommendations for each of the five topic areas, plus cross-cutting themes such as education. While the French, Scottish and Irish Biodiversity Loss assemblies added extra time at the request of their members, they had the resources to support the additional work. In Luxembourg, the organisers had to design a second phase from scratch with no extra resources.

Facilitation

The change in facilitation styles that was forced on the Luxembourg process out of necessity mirrors differences within facilitation philosophy and practice. Democratic lottery generates a group of members who differ widely in terms of their confidence and willingness to speak in front of others. Those who favour more directive table facilitation do so with the objective of promoting equality between members. Facilitators work with small number of participants on tables, creating the space to ensure reflection on each other's experience, on the input from witnesses, on the selection of questions for witnesses, on the development of ideas and on refining recommendations. Facilitators play a critical role in ensuring that all members feel able to contribute and are heard.

For some organisers, particularly in Denmark and France, a different philosophy and practice of facilitation is applied. More emphasis is placed on promoting the autonomy and collective empowerment and creativity of members. A smaller number of facilitators will oversee table conversations, but from a distance, allowing members to self-organise their work. Facilitators will step in if groups become dysfunctional and to ensure members keep to tasks.

Denmark and France also place more power in the hands of members to shape the evidence they engage with. In Denmark, for example, members select the topics they wish to hear about from witnesses, again drawing from their experience with consensus conferences. The French are unusual in allowing members to work directly with experts and advocates in the development of proposals, to the extent that the Convention's working methods have been referred to as 'co-construction'.[8]

The French introduced another innovation, appointing a group of legal experts to provide detailed guidance to members to turn their proposals into a form that could be presented as a law, regulation or referendum as requested by the President. Other assemblies have introduced reviews of draft recommendations to give members a sense of how they might be strengthened to have more impact on commissioners and stakeholders. For example, in Denmark, two external experts, with experience in energy modelling and public administration, provided feedback before members prepared their final recommendations. The power, though, rests with members to decide whether to accept the advice given.

The working practices of the French Convention were generally laxer than other assemblies in policing boundaries. Not only did experts and advocates work directly with members on some of the recommendations, but members of the Governance Committee and Guarantors broke with the principle of independence on more than one occasion, expressing strong political positions within the assembly itself and in the media. Those empowered to take on governance roles did not retain the distance from the deliberations of the assembly that is generally expected. This may have compromised the integrity of governance, but it also meant more media attention and thus public knowledge and understanding of the assembly.

Public Communication and Engagement

How can assemblies make sure that wider publics understand what they are doing? The resources put into communication strategies varies widely. The Austrians and French spent as much as €1 million, whereas the Danes had no communication budget. Those with resources have been able to build relationships with journalists and other media actors. The Austrian, French and Ireland's Biodiversity Loss assemblies have experimented with working closely with social media influencers to extend their reach.

Assemblies vary in the extent to which they protect the identities of members. Because of their concerns about personal safety in relation to the abortion issue, the Irish are probably the most protective. The French offered the most access to journalists, but only to those members who were willing to engage. Some of the members became well known faces and voices in traditional and new media.

Austria introduced three innovations, all of which aimed to bring the assembly into conversation with broader society. First, it created opportunities for the members of its Stakeholder Advisory Board to engage directly with assembly members. Second, two civil society engagement officers led more in-depth communication with interested institutions and organisations. Third, the wider public was invited to engage with ideas emerging from the assembly's workstreams on the digital crowdsourcing platform Pol.is. We will have more to say about these developments later in the book.

Reports and Recommendations

Assemblies tend to use simple voting procedures on recommendations, reporting the percentage for and against each one. The potential for experimentation with more sophisticated approaches to decision making has not really been explored.

Climate Assembly UK is the only assembly divided into workstreams where members could vote only on the policy options within their streams: a decision based on ensuring the vote was as informed as possible. In other assemblies, it is noticeable how trusting assembly members are of their peers who have worked on very different policy areas. Support tends to be high across most proposals.

Reports generally combine a vision statement agreed by the assembly, alongside recommendations. From its experience with consensus conferences and other deliberative processes, the Danish Board of Technology provided a template to assembly members that required an observation and assessment of the current situation alongside the recommendation. The report then clarifies the rationale for each proposal so that it is more difficult for commissioners and others to misinterpret the intentions of the assembly.

The number of recommendations varies considerably: from the 13 recommendations on climate policy from the first Irish Citizens' Assembly to the staggering 172 from the Spanish Citizens' Assembly for the Climate. Debate rages amongst practitioners as to whether it is better to require assembly members to prioritise a relatively small number of recommendations – the argument being that it is easier to monitor the response to a more limited number of proposals – or whether this is an unreasonable restriction on members.

Official Response

What are governments obliged to do on receiving an assembly's report? In rare cases a legal commitment exists for a response from the commissioner to the report and recommendations within a certain time frame. In Scotland, the law required that the government must respond within six months. In Ireland the parliamentary regulation for the Citizens' Assembly on Biodiversity Loss states that the report must be considered by a joint committee of both houses of parliament, followed by a government response. No specific dates are fixed.

In most other circumstances a more informal promise is made to the assembly, which is not always realised. For example, in Austria, the promised official response from the government was never forthcoming because of differences that emerged between coalition partners. Only a review of the relationship between assembly recommendations and current government policy was produced by the administration. We have more to say about follow-up in the next chapter.

Monitoring

How do we make sure that assembly recommendations are treated seriously by commissioning bodies? In most assemblies, some members will engage with the government while it is considering how to deal with the recommendations. Specific support is generally provided to help build the capacity of members to meet with public officials. It is after all a very different experience from participating in an assembly. In Spain, for example, the NGO Red Esapñola para el Desarrollo Sostenible was funded by the European Climate Foundation to undertake this capacity building role.

The French Convention and Scotland's Climate Assembly are the only two national assemblies that reconvened a few months after delivering their reports to review the government's response.

In Austria and France, many of the assembly members formed civic organisations to collectively monitor government action. In both cases, the members found it challenging to move from the facilitated context of an assembly to autonomous self-organisation and to sustain the same levels of diversity – one of the defining features of the assembly.

In Ireland, no expectations are placed on assembly members to engage with the government. It is the Chair that takes on this responsibility.

Sub-National Innovation

Many of these differences in practice between assemblies at national level are found amongst municipal and regional climate assemblies. Given the larger numbers of sub-national assemblies, it is no surprise that we can find interesting innovations in practice. Three examples will suffice for now.

Almost all citizens' assemblies (whether on the climate and ecological crisis or other policy areas) are advisory in nature. A small number of Polish municipal assemblies have bucked this trend and have been empowered to make decisions. In these cities, the mayor committed to implement proposals where a near consensus is achieved within the assembly – over 80 per cent support amongst members. Not surprisingly this practice has not spread, given how reluctant politicians generally are to give away power.

A second innovation, in the German city of Erlangen, brings stakeholders and scientific experts into conversation with a climate assembly in a different way. Proposals moved between a local research institute, a stakeholder forum and the assembly in three cycles of development. We will have more to say about this example in Chapter 3.

In Brussels and Milan, we have witnessed the establishment of permanent climate assemblies. In those two municipalities, the membership and the specific remits change every year. Their modes of operation are different, which we will explore further in Chapter 4. The emergence of permanent bodies is a potential step change for climate assembly practice.

What this dive into assembly practice shows us is that climate assemblies can have some quite profound differences. Their family resemblance rests on selection by democratic lottery and facilitated deliberation. Beyond those core features, significant diversity exists in the way that assemblies are designed and delivered. Some more successfully than others.

No perfect assembly design exists, but as our knowledge of what works develops, hopefully mistakes can be avoided and more robust practice sustained.

What Citizens Want

We now have hundreds of recommendations from climate assemblies. What does this tell us about what citizens want? Consistently they want more action by governments and stakeholders. Their recommendations are generally more ambitious than existing government policy, with much more focus on restraining consumption and production and more willingness to apply the regulatory power of the state.

Assemblies bring into sharp focus inconsistencies in government action. The French think tank, IDRRI, argues that the Convention:

> broke the silence surrounding the contradictions of current policies. For example, how can airport expansions be planned and carbon neutrality pursued when the technological solutions are still highly uncertain? How can people accept higher fuel taxes for land-based mobility when the air transport sector is exonerated from such taxes?[9]

When it takes an interest in assemblies, the media likes to court controversy. It tends to spotlight those recommendations that are most politically divisive and would have significant direct effect on the lives and aspirations of the public. Recommendations to restrict flying, car driving and the consumption of meat and dairy tend to hit the headlines. These are issues that assembly members have been willing to tackle head on. Unlike their governments.

One of the iconic recommendations from the French Convention is the proposal to end domestic flights by 2025 where a low-carbon alternative exists that takes less than four hours. It received 88 per cent support within the assembly. Climate Assembly UK proposed taxes that increase as people fly more often and fly further (this received 80 per cent support) and in Scotland the call was to introduce a frequent flyer tax or levy (which achieved 78 per cent support) and eliminate frequent flyer bonuses (92 per cent). These are not proposals that scraped through. They had significant majority support from members.

Similarly for diet, one of the objectives of the French Convention, supported by 93 per cent of members, is to promote 'a healthy, sustainable, less animal and more plant-based diet, respectful of production, low greenhouse gas emissions and accessible to all'. The Danish assembly proposed increasing demand for plant-based foods, for example, through incentive schemes or taxes on animal-based products to reduce meat consumption (83 per cent) and the introduction of new dietary recommendations to minimise meat consumption (81 per cent). The Germans also proposed awareness campaigns promoting avoidance of meat and dairy (76 per cent) and a ban on advertising climate damaging and unhealthy foods (94 per cent). The Austrian assembly similarly proposed incentives for climate-friendly diets to reduce meat consumption and food waste (98 per cent).

Sufficiency and Regulation

Picking out air travel and diet is instructive, but it does not answer the question of whether and how the recommendations of assemblies are systematically different from the policies adopted by governments. A recent study compares national climate assembly recommendations to the policies in the National Energy and

Climate Plans (NECPs) that Member States are required to adopt by the European Commission.[10] Researcher Jonas Lage and his colleagues find two patterns.

First, assemblies are braver than governments in their willingness to recommend policies that aim to reduce consumption and production of products and services. These are referred to as 'sufficiency' policies. Second, citizens are more willing to propose the regulation of individuals and businesses rather than relying on market incentives or voluntary action.

The types of policy proposals associated with restricting air travel and diets fit this pattern. So do proposals from the German assembly for prolonging the lifetime of electric appliances, with a minimum warranty time of ten years and obligations for manufacturers to provide replacement parts (91 per cent were in favour). Or the Austrian proposals to restrict advertisements for products with negative climate impact and a ban on all highly damaging goods (100 per cent support) and the reduction of standard work week to four days to reduce commuting trips (93 per cent voted in support).

This difference between assemblies and governments is not trivial. Assemblies are three to six times more likely to propose limits on consumption and production compared to their governments. Similarly, assemblies propose regulatory policies three times more often.

Summarising their findings, the authors of the study argue that climate assemblies tend to be 'more open towards innovative and potentially controversial topics'. They are willing to confront consumption and production rather than relying on high-tech solutions such as geoengineering. Assemblies are unafraid to support the regulatory power of the state.

Removal of Greenhouse Gases

What do assemblies have to say about often controversial policies to remove greenhouse gases? Climate Assembly UK is an example of the scepticism of members towards government strategies to rely on technical fixes for removal. Technologies such as bioenergy and direct air carbon capture and storage did not get majority support, with assembly members concerned that they are 'treated as [a] magic solution' that 'takes the focus off the amount that we are emitting in the first place.'[11] While they recognised that removal methods are a necessary part of how the UK reaches net zero, members placed more emphasis on forestry, peatland and wetland restoration and management, the use of wood in construction and enhancing the storage of carbon. Such methods were attractive because they have significant co-benefits associated with enhanced biodiversity, flood and erosion prevention and access to nature.

Systems Transformation

Most assembly recommendations are specific to particular policy areas, primarily because this is the way that assemblies are organised, a theme we pick up in Chapter 4. Even so, their approach in these areas can be transformational. As the IDDRI report on the French Convention shows, the citizens adopted a 'systems approach to mobility' that did not simply make the case for electric vehicles but recognised that decarbonisation must be accompanied by reconsiderations of modes of personal and goods transport and land use, while guaranteeing social justice.[12]

Constitutional recommendations are often transformational in character. The French Convention proposed to change the preamble of the constitution, 'reinforcing France's responsibility in preserving biodiversity, the environment and the fight for climate change'. It also proposed 'constitutionalising environmental control, which could be exercised by a new body: a "defender of the environment"'.[13]

The recent Irish Citizens' Assembly on Biodiversity Loss has recommended a change to the constitution, not only to secure human environmental rights, but also rights of nature.[14] Substantive rights for nature would recognise 'nature as a holder of legal rights, comparable to companies or people e.g., to exist, flourish/perpetuate and be restored if degraded; not to be polluted/harmed/degraded'. Procedural rights would enable nature 'to be a party in administrative decision-making, litigation, etc. where rights are impacted/likely to be impacted'. In principle, such constitutional change would shift the burden of proof onto polluters to show that their activities do no undue harm and provide legal avenues for the protection of nature. This could have profound affects on the way we organise our society and economy.

In Scotland, one of the goals set by the assembly is to reframe how we understand progress, a statement supported by 83 per cent of members:

> Reframe the national focus and vision for Scotland's future away from economic growth and Gross Domestic Product (GDP) in order to reflect climate change goals towards the prioritisation of a more person and community centred vision of thriving people, thriving communities and thriving climate.[15]

Throughout their reports, it is noticeable how often assembly members refer to questions of fairness and the just distribution of costs and benefits for the transition. Some assemblies make explicit reference to fairness or justice in their remits (France, Scotland, Spain). Others ensure evidence is provided on these issues. More than their governments, assembly recommendations are sensitive to the impact that climate action can have on the poorest and marginalised within society and are keen to protect their interests. At the same time, those with high consumption lifestyles are seen as fair targets for bearing more of the costs of transition.

Overlooked Policy Areas

The coverage of proposals tends be skewed towards some areas of policy over others. The largest sectoral emitter of greenhouse gases in Europe is energy production and supply and yet only 15 per cent of recommendations from the first eight national assemblies are in this area of policy. Relatively few assemblies have had a workstream specifically focused on energy. Where it is considered, it is very much related to household and transport energy use. Very little attention has been given to questions of energy production and supply.

Similarly, just over 1 per cent of recommendations focused on finance. That fundamental element of the contemporary economy has been almost entirely overlooked.

Much of the explanation rests on how the workstreams of the assemblies have been defined. Most focus attention on those elements of climate that have direct impact on the lives of citizens, with transport and mobility generating the highest number of recommendations. It is a missed opportunity to bring the shared wisdom and common sense of citizens to bear on systems of provision that structure our everyday lives.

The Impact of Climate Assemblies

Climate assemblies propose more ambitious policy, but does this translate into action? What impacts have climate assemblies had? The tendency is to focus on the effect of assemblies on climate policy. Given that the majority of assemblies are commissioned by government, such policy impact is a reasonable expectation. But we should not only limit our consideration of policy effects.[16]

Impacts can take different forms beyond policy (see Figure 2.3). Climate assemblies can have effects on institutions and actors. Not just on government and other state institutions, but also non-state

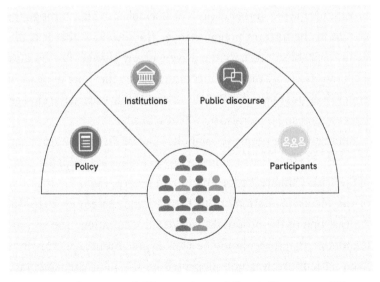

Figure 2.3: Impacts of Climate Assemblies © European Climate Foundation.

actors such as civil society organisations, private companies, the media and broader publics. They can impact upon social and economic structures and systems, although these are harder to shift.

These impacts may not just be instrumental: on specific policies, attitudes and behaviours. They can also be conceptual impacts on the way we understand and think about climate action or even impacts that increase our capacity to respond to the climate and ecological crisis through the creation of new institutions and ways of working.

Impact on Policy

Judging the effect on policy of climate assemblies is difficult for two reasons. The first is that policy impact can take time. Most assemblies have only happened in the last few years and it can be a slow process for the recommendations of assemblies to filter through the system in the form of policy change. The second is that it is difficult to establish precisely the drivers of any change. Just because a climate assembly makes a recommendation that later appears in policy does not mean that it is the assembly that caused the change. Other actors and dynamics may be responsible.

While evidence of impact on policy can be difficult to trace and has varied between assemblies, a few examples are palpable.

The Irish Climate Action Bill (2020) incorporated the majority of the recommendations from the Citizens' Assembly 2016–18. At least one of the proposals was lost in translation. The recommendation that there should be a tax on greenhouse gas emissions from agriculture was not supported by the joint parliamentary committee on climate action. It was seen as one step too far in antagonising the powerful farming interests in Ireland. Even so, the assembly is widely recognised as played a critical role in Ireland's step change from being a laggard on climate policy.

The debate over the impact on policy of the French Convention rages. The newspaper *Le Monde* is scathing in its assessment, whereas the government's tracking website suggests a high degree of legal translation of recommendations into law and policy. The truth is somewhere in between. What is clear is that the Convention's report and its recommendations were the subject of a lobbying offensive from potentially affected industries, including aviation, agrochemicals and advertising, and resistance from many politicians and public officials.[17]

Against this highly politicised backdrop, a recent study suggests that around 20 per cent of the assembly's recommendations were fully implemented or even reinforced, with 15 per cent abandoned.[18] Just shy of 60 per cent have been translated into law in a modified form. For example, the government accepted the proposal to end domestic flights where a low-carbon alternative exists but restricted the ban to journeys of less than two hours compared to the Convention's recommendation of four hours. Other recommendations that had proposed government regulation were converted to voluntary or incentive-based instruments.

The analysis provides evidence that the government did not simply implement those recommendations that it was already considering. The intervention of the Convention appears to have changed hearts and minds to some degree.

More recently, a number of the recommendations of the Luxembourg Climate Citizens' Council have been translated into the redrafted National Energy and Climate Plan submitted to the European Commission. The Council had been established for that purpose and is responsible for five new measures being added, with 19 existing measures strengthened. Other measures are still being assessed and some require European or international agreement.

Impact on Institutions and Climate Actors

Have the impacts of climate assemblies reverberated further through the political system? Have they changed the ways that key climate institutions and actors think about climate and citizen engagement?

Climate Assembly UK was commissioned by parliamentary select committees and recognisably increased the capacity of at least one committee to effectively scrutinise government action on climate. Perhaps more significant has been its impact on the UK Climate Change Committee. The Committee is an independent, statutory body established under the Climate Change Act 2008 which committed the UK to achieve net zero by 2050. It advises the UK and devolved governments on emissions targets and reports to Parliament on the progress made in reducing greenhouse gas emissions and preparing for and adapting to the impacts of climate change.

The Climate Change Committee used Climate Assembly UK's recommendations to frame its Sixth Carbon Budget, reviewing government policy in relation to the proposals. The UK assembly was also a stimulus for the Committee to consider how to further integrate deliberative methods into its work. For example, it commissioned its own citizens' panel on home decarbonisation.[19] The effect on the Committee is an example of an assembly having direct instrumental impact, but also conceptual and capacity effects.

This newfound enthusiasm for deliberative processes can be traced to the role that Chris Stark, the Climate Change Committee's

Chief Executive, played as an Expert Lead for Climate Assembly UK. Stark has talked about his trepidation in taking on this role and his arrogance in wondering what citizens could add to climate governance. Taking part challenged his prejudices: 'I had a totally game changing experience ... I felt we had a genuinely representative group of people and were taking them through some difficult issues, ones which we struggled with in our technical work.'[20]

We should not forget the transformative effect assemblies can have on those more seasoned individuals and organisations involved in their planning and delivery. This is one of the reasons why organisers are so keen for key politicians, policy officials and stakeholders to attend assemblies. Seeing citizens in action can have a profound effect on often sceptical attitudes towards assemblies in a way that reading a report (or a book!) cannot.

Another example of the way that assemblies can build capacity in climate governance takes us back to Ireland. It is common practice for joint committees from both Houses of Parliament to be created to review the recommendations from citizens' assemblies. The original assembly report and the report from the committee are then presented to government at which point the committee ceases to exist. The Joint Parliamentary Committee on Climate Action was thus one in a series of committees established following a citizens' assembly. What is different is that having considered the Irish Citizens' Assembly's recommendations on climate, parliament decided to make the Committee a permanent body. In other words, the assembly directly led to the creation of a new piece of climate governance architecture.

A final example of how assemblies can have institutional impacts comes from Denmark. As part of its response to the

Danish Climate Assembly's report, the government gave the assembly the same status as social partnerships that are established within different social and economic sectors. In Danish politics, it is a requirement to consult social partners when policy and legislation is likely to affect their interests. Similarly, then, when policy is being developed that relates to recommendations that emerged from the Danish assembly, it is expected that these will be fully considered within decision making. It is not clear, however, how this will operate practically.

Impact on Public Discourse

For some advocates of citizens' assemblies, their primary impact should be on the wider public. It should help inform and change the dynamics of public and political debate. But, most assemblies have failed to resonate with the broader public. It is not because of a lack of interest in this new form of participation. Survey experiments suggest quite extensive support. When people are aware of assemblies or introduced to the idea of one, levels of trust, confidence and perceived legitimacy tend to be higher than for other political institutions.[21] The problem is that assemblies have not been picked up by the media (established or new). Without media attention, public attention is highly unlikely.

Two assemblies have broken through and enjoyed significant levels of media attention and public recognition. Both invested a significant proportion of their budget and time into communication.

The Austrian Citizens' Climate Council was reported in both national and regional newspapers and radio stations. By the end of the process, over 50 per cent of the population had heard of the assembly with over 90 per cent finding out via the media. A large majority of citizens were in favour of the assembly and wanted political actors to use its recommendations as a yardstick for climate policy.[22] The failure of the government to respond to the assembly did generate some media attention, but it soon drifted away.

It is the French Convention that is unusual in stimulating extensive public debate on both climate transition and the use of assemblies. The Convention played a significant role in raising the profile and salience of climate as an issue that could not be ignored by politicians. A number of factors may help explain this broader public engagement. First, the context: the Convention took place against the background of social unrest. Second, the level of political engagement by the President increased public attention. He publicly called the Convention into being, promised 'no filter' for recommendations, spoke at and was questioned at one of its sessions and received the report in the garden of his official residency. Third, the organisers of the assembly were themselves active in engaging the media throughout. As part of that strategy, they supported those assembly members willing to engage directly with media outlets. Other assemblies have tended to be more protective of their members and organisers and those in governance bodies have been more restrained in making public pronouncements.

The Convention did not only raise the level of public debate on climate but paved the way for further assemblies across France at different levels of governance. It was the blueprint for a second national Convention, this time on end of life.

In Ireland, where citizens' assemblies are a more familiar part of the political landscape, media interest tends to be higher and so assemblies have more potential to shift public discourse. Fintan Kelly from the Irish Environment Network was 'originally sceptical' of the Citizens' Assembly on Biodiversity Loss, concerned that 'it would just be a talking shop'. But his opinion shifted:

> The Assemblies [adult and children and young people] have helped to elevate the importance of biodiversity loss within Irish politics. I would say before that, biodiversity loss was more of a niche issue within politics and in recent decades it has been the poor cousin of climate change in terms of prioritisation and media attention ... The Citizens Assembly also established a powerful public mandate for action which has already helped to secure government support for a National Nature Restoration Plan.[23]

Impact on Assembly Members

Finally, we must not forget the impact assemblies have on their members. They have gone through a process unlike any other in their lives. What does it do to them?

Almost without exception, a significant majority of members of climate assemblies find the process transformative. This is the case whether they participate in a large-scale national (or even transnational) assembly or a smaller local one. Even those less well organised processes report strong effects. We should not underestimate the power of the invitation to do something unusual. As a result of taking part, members increase their political efficacy and desire to engage further with climate and other political and community activities.

Some of the stories that come out from assemblies are incredibly inspiring. Rebecca Lester, one of the members of the People's Assembly on Nature in the UK, has talked movingly about the effect of participating on her life. She is now one of the most active advocates of the People's Plan for Nature, speaking at events as diverse as business conferences and Extinction Rebellions protests.

> In the weeks running up to the first weekend, the amount of elaborate lies I concocted in my head as to why I couldn't attend, was ridiculous. The assembly was going to take place in Birmingham. Getting to Birmingham, mentally, was incredibly hard. My mental health has been a struggle for a few years now, and socialising, even with friends, is something I avoid. Yet, something made me push through and turn up. I am so glad I did … Beyond creating the People's Plan for Nature itself, it has opened up numerous opportunities for me … Feeling a part of something bigger, something that mattered, has helped me rediscover a part of myself that I had lost. I will always be grateful. Together, humans are capable of amazing things, and when personal agendas and politics are removed, we can create truly amazing things.[24]

Important evidence has emerged that these effects on members are not as transient as some had feared. A survey undertaken two years after the launch of the Climate Assembly UK report found strong and consistent effects on the attitudes and behaviours of members towards climate action that is sustained and even enhanced over time.[25] Assembly members' concern about climate change continued to increase after the assembly. At the start of the assembly, 46 per cent of members stated they were 'very concerned' about climate change, a similar rate to those in the broader population. By the end of the assembly this figure had risen to 56 per cent. Two years later it stood at 74 per cent, significantly higher than the broader population.

The survey found that many assembly members had made changes to their lives once the assembly had ended. These ranged from paying more attention to climate change in the news and discussing climate change more with people around them to reducing the amount of meat and dairy in their diets and electricity use in their homes.

These changes are spread evenly across assembly members, with no statistical differences emerging for age, ethnicity, level of education, left-right ideological orientation and attitudes towards climate change at the start of the assembly. This is a particularly encouraging finding. Those most sceptical towards climate action at the start of the process are just as likely to shift their attitudes and behaviours over time.

The one area where attitudes shifted in a more negative direction is in relation to the political system. Members' belief that Climate Assembly UK's recommendations would influence parliament and government dropped markedly as did their belief that they had a say in what the UK parliament does and how well the UK system works. This should not be a surprise given the lack of direct and obvious effects of the assembly's recommendations on policy. Even against this backdrop of political disillusionment, their support for the use of citizens' assemblies remains high.

CHAPTER 3

Enhancing Impact

Climate assemblies provide a rare space within which everyday people exercise their collective judgement on the climate and ecological challenges we face as a society. We see consistent transformative effects on their members but inconsistent impact on climate policy and governance and broader public discourse. What can we learn from the first wave of assemblies to enhance and sustain the impact of future assemblies?

Our focus in this chapter is on how we can increase the impact of climate assemblies commissioned by government. This is the standard operating model for assemblies. Most of the 'deliberative wave' has been established by public authorities with the express intention of affecting climate policy and governance. How can we enhance the impact of this model?

A simple way of expressing the problem we face goes back to the reason why assemblies are organised in the first place. Politicians and civil servants recognise the dysfunctionality of their response to the climate and ecological crisis and so commission an assembly. They recognise the importance of creating a space for citizens protected from the dynamics of electoral and administrative politics. But then what happens? The assembly proposes a set of robust recommendations that are sent back into the dysfunctional system. Under these conditions, perhaps we should be surprised that assemblies have any impact at all!

This chapter considers four areas that are critical to enhancing the impact of assemblies on climate governance: remit; follow-up; stakeholder involvement; and public communication and engagement. Getting these elements right does not guarantee impact on the policy system or broader public discourse. But it does increase the chances of this happening.

The first element is asking the right question: getting the remit right. This may seem an odd place to start when it comes to impact, but if you don't ask the right question, then the answer is likely to be of little use. Most national assemblies have put very broad questions to members. Municipal and regional assemblies have often adopted tighter agendas focused on particular policy challenges. Which is the right way to go?

Second, how do we make sure that recommendations are taken seriously within the sponsoring body? What needs to be put in place within public authorities to ensure that reports and recommendations are followed up and don't just gather dust on a shelf?

The third element broadens this question of follow-up, recognising that it is not only public authorities that need to respond to assemblies. A number of the recommendations of assemblies will require other institutions and agencies to act beyond the public authority. How to encourage stakeholders that have not commissioned the assembly to take its recommendations seriously?

And finally, how to overcome the gap between those participating in the assembly and wider publics outside? If one of the motivations for organising assemblies is to increase the legitimacy and public acceptance of climate and ecological action, then a precondition is that the public know about these processes and their outcomes. But journalists and media platforms are not familiar with assemblies. How can we communicate this novel form of democracy and engage larger numbers beyond those selected by democratic lottery?

If governments and organisers get these four elements right then they can open up pathways to impact for climate assemblies.

Getting the Remit Right

We are faced with an all-encompassing climate and ecological crisis. As we saw in the last chapter, the response of most commissioners at the national level has been to establish remits that ask assemblies to deal with this interconnected set of challenges. These have been broad remits focused on greenhouse gas mitigation and at times adaptation. A number have asked assembly members to do this while also considering the implications for social justice. This is quite a mandate.

At national level, it is only the Polish Citizens' Assembly that chose a tighter remit, asking how the specific problem of energy poverty can be counteracted.

We find a more mixed approach at municipal and regional levels. While many remits are similarly broad, tighter remits are more common than at national level, with assemblies established to deal with specific climate and ecological policy challenges and dilemmas such as flooding or air pollution.

Figure 3.1: Poland's Citizens' Assembly on Energy Costs
© Wojciech Radwanski/Fundacja Stocznia.

Figure 3.1: Continued.

These stark differences in remits have generated lively debate about the most effective approach. Broad or tight?[1]

Questions also emerge about who gets to set the remit. The working assumption is that if the government commissions the process, it decides the question. A few cases have challenged this assumption.

Broad or Tight?

Broad remits give assemblies a mandate to develop an overarching platform for climate action that cuts across different policy areas. In principle, it gives members more freedom to respond to the remit on their own terms and in so doing can generate a strong sense of ownership of the agenda. Broad remits open up the potential to deal with systemic issues, in particular interconnections and interdependencies between policy areas – for example, that transport policies do not have a negative impact on energy policies, land-use, biodiversity, and so on.

A tighter remit means that members are able to focus more attention on current policy dilemmas where specific policy windows are open: i.e., those moments when opportunities exist to redefine problems and policies.[2] A more detailed package of policy proposals can be generated that are relevant to the immediate needs of policy makers and where it is easier to hold the authority to account for its response.

A more prosaic reason for tighter remits is that in some political contexts, climate change and climate action are highly contested and polarising issues. Organisers have managed to avoid the high levels of political contestation associated with climate through a focus on more specific policy areas that enjoy a broader consensus. This was the reason why the Shipyard Foundation used the framing of energy poverty for the nationwide Polish assembly. Similarly, the climate assembly in Skopje in North Macedonia primarily focused on air pollution – an issue that is recognised as salient across party political divisions.

The effectiveness of broader remits has been mixed, as we saw in the last chapter. Organisers do not have endless resources and members cannot give up endless time. As such, many assemblies have been split into workstreams to deal with the broad agenda. Given time and resource constraints, such an approach is completely understandable. But this means that while the assembly as a whole has a broad agenda, members then work within policy silos. In practice, then, many large-scale climate assemblies break up into smaller assemblies with different policy remits. Organisers work hard to ensure opportunities for the different workstreams to share their ideas and draft proposals, but members are still predominately working within distinct policy areas.

Certain issues slip off the agenda. We have already seen that in France energy generation was not an explicit element of any of the workstreams. And early conversations that emerged about the nature of Gross Domestic Product (GDP) as a driver of the current growth model did not fit within a workstream. Members can think systematically, but the structures of the assemblies may themselves constrain that thinking. We will pick up this theme of systems thinking in Chapter 4 as it is worth more sustained consideration.

One way that a small number of organisers have managed the time challenges of broad agendas is to task the assembly with reviewing policy options or scenarios developed in advance by climate experts. Both Climate Assembly UK and Finland's Citizens' Jury on Climate Actions took this approach. It is highly responsive to the commissioner's immediate policy needs but leaves much less space for members to be creative.

A further challenge of broad remits is that assemblies often generate a large number of policy proposals. One hundred and seventy-two in the case of Spain. One hundred and fifty-nine on biodiversity loss in Ireland. It is not necessarily the case. Ireland's Citizens' Assembly 2016–18 generated only 13 recommendations. Most assemblies have not actively limited the number of recommendations they produce. This can be a challenge to commissioning authorities and other stakeholders. Different areas of policy will be at different points in the policy cycle. For some, the policy window will be ajar and the policy process receptive to input. Others will not be open to policy development. Rarely is the whole of climate policy open at the same time given that it cuts across so many different policy arenas. A large number of proposals also opens up space for the commissioning body to cherry-pick those recommendations that fit with existing policies and strategies.

But tight remits generate their own challenges. It tends to be more difficult to deal with interconnections between policy areas and other systemic challenges when focused on specific policy issues in isolation. And assembly members can sometimes feel constrained by an agenda that is more obviously aimed at fulfilling the specific needs of the commissioning authority.

The broad versus tight debate needs to be placed in context. Some broad remits are tied to specific policy development opportunities – to moments when commissioners are open to input from citizens. For example, the broad remit of the Danish Climate Assembly was explicitly linked to the government's annual climate action planning process. In Luxembourg, the assembly was commissioned to consider the revision of its National Energy and Climate Plan. In Ireland, the broad agenda was offered in recognition of the government's relatively poor performance on climate policy compared to other European nations. The broad remit had a specific landing point within the public administration.

Other assemblies have not been the product of an overt government need. For example, the broad remit of the Austrian Citizens' Climate Council was the result of public demand expressed through a citizens' initiative.

The explicit linking of assembly to policy making opportunity does not necessarily lead to direct policy impact. The impact in Denmark is much less than in Ireland and Luxembourg. Other factors, such as high-level political support and the design of follow-up, are just as important explanatory factors, if not more so.

Who Sets the Remit?

In Denmark's Citizens' Assembly on Climate, a broad remit was established by the government asking the assembly to inform the process of transition and the national climate plan. Within that remit, assembly members were empowered to prioritise the areas they wished to focus on. Remember that the Danish assembly is the only one that was organised across two phases – to experiment with different approaches. The prioritisation happened in different ways in the two phases.

In the first phase, members defined their workstreams having spent time learning in some depth about climate change and the challenges facing Denmark. In the second phase, when two-thirds of the members had been replaced with new members, the organisers experimented with prioritisation without prior input. In retrospect, the organisers felt that the first phase was more effective, where citizens had developed a collective understanding of the current context before defining their workstreams.

The Danish assembly raises the question of the extent to which citizens or other actors aside from government should be empowered to shape the scope of the remit. Generally, the remit is set by the sponsoring body and the organisers and governance bodies then establish the structure and content of the assembly work programme. But exceptions have emerged.

The permanent Brussels Climate Assembly empowers members to decide on the remit, but in a different way to the Danish experience. Assembly members are replaced on an annual basis and it is a group of those who are leaving the assembly who set the remit for the next one, having consulted with the municipal authority and other stakeholders. This has the advantage that those setting the agenda have direct experience of being in a climate assembly, so they have a better idea of what works in this context. We will have more to say about the Brussels assembly in the next chapter.

Other assemblies have given a distinct role to stakeholders. The remit of Scotland's Climate Assembly was broadly framed through legislation, but the specific question asked of the assembly was decided through a series of facilitated workshops involving members of the assembly's stakeholder Stewarding Group and the Secretariat of seconded civil servants.

The Devon Climate Assembly in the UK was preceded by a consultation exercise with stakeholders and the public which narrowed the remit down to three widely recognised policy challenges: renewable energy, car use and the retrofitting of buildings.

Giving members and stakeholders a role in defining the remit can certainly increase their agency and buy-in to the process.

The balance is potentially between their empowerment and policy relevance to the sponsoring body. Where that balance lies is as much a philosophical question as it is practical.

Broad or tight? Agenda set by commission authority, citizens or stakeholders?

Such decisions can have profound effects on the impact of assemblies. Which is the right way to go? Much depends on context and what is trying to be achieved. Many things are being balanced when a remit is established.

- A remit needs to be timely, taking into account whether policy windows are open.
- It needs to be relevant for both citizens and commissioners.
- It needs to be responsive to the context of climate politics in a particular jurisdiction.
- It needs to be accepted by most stakeholders.
- It needs to be sensitive to constraints of time and money.

How these considerations are best balanced will vary. No single right answer emerges. It's a question of judgement. At times a broad remit will be most relevant. At other times, a tighter remit will make more sense. At times, a remit can be tied tightly to particular policy needs of commissioning authorities. At other times, a more open agenda will make more sense, with more emphasis on empowering citizens' and stakeholders' choice.

Box 3.1: Lessons for the Remit.

Designing Follow-Up

The biggest worry about citizens' assemblies is that they are just 'talking shops' with no impact on climate governance. If this is the case, citizens will soon cotton on, losing interest and potentially becoming hostile to this democratic innovation. It will be a wasted opportunity to do something different and productive.

The challenge then is how to ensure that the recommendations of assemblies are seriously considered by commissioning authorities? How to design effective follow-up? The relatively limited and inconsistent impact on policy to date suggests that assemblies are too often poorly integrated with political and administrative systems.

Some advocates of assemblies have an unreasonable expectation of the impact of assemblies. The assumption that the 'moral force' of the recommendations from a citizens' assembly is enough to generate policy change is naïve at best. Assemblies are a new intervention in the political system and policy can be notoriously difficult to shift, not least because of the power of vested interests within and beyond government that are resistant to change.

The failure to follow up the recommendations of assemblies can be understood in two ways. One is a clash of operational logics. The second is more prosaic: a failure to design, resource and prioritise follow-up.

Operational Logics

What do we mean by a clash of operational logics?[3] The new practice of citizen deliberation encompasses a range of expectations that differ from those of electoral politics and public administration. The promise of doing politics differently comes into direct tension with the conflicting logics of established electoral and bureaucratic ways of doing things. These are the very logics that are implicated in our current climate and ecological crisis.

Bureaucratic logic places a premium on hierarchical account-ability, specialised expertise and the routinisation of tasks. Chris Stark, CEO of the UK Climate Change Committee, is open about why many of his colleagues within climate governance networks are at best cautious of assemblies, not knowing what status to give the recommendations of assemblies:

> The basic reaction you get from the policy profession is that this isn't "real" data. I think we in the CCC [Climate Change Committee] have that attitude as well – there's no point denying it. I think that's the hardest thing to overcome because it's essentially cultural. Central government is even worse. It's quite tricky to overcome, but I think it's important that we try.[4]

In comparison, electoral logic places a premium on political compe-tition and party differentiation. We have too many examples where one political party becomes associated with an assembly, which is then used as a wedge issue by other parties keen to score political points. The Austrian Citizens' Climate Council was quickly asso-ciated with government ministers from the Green Party, with its conservative coalition partner, the People's Party, distancing itself from the initiative and using its opposition for political advantage.

Bureaucrats and politicians often see assemblies as an illegiti-mate challenge to their professional status and political authority. A member of parliamentary staff recounts the resistance of Mem-bers of Parliament towards Climate Assembly UK:

> Some MPs were more dubious about it, partly because they really didn't know much about citizens assemblies,

> but also the instant response from many MPs was, why
> do we need the Citizens Assembly? We are the Citizens
> Assembly. We're elected parliamentarians.[5]

For deliberative processes like assemblies to be effective, they require political representatives and bureaucrats to provide the necessary political support, resources and expert input to enable citizen deliberation. But they also have to be open to considering recommendations developed by citizens that may run counter to current policy and ways of working, and which may be difficult to sell electorally. That is a lot to ask. Particularly given the power of vested interests in these arenas.

One way that organisers have worked to change the perspective of policy actors – whether elected representatives or bureaucrats – has been to invite them to observe the assembly. Widely held prejudices about the capacity of citizens and questions about the value of the assembly process tend to dissolve when they see the members in action.

It is also increasingly common for assembly members to meet with policy actors after the assembly to promote and explain their recommendations.[6] This first-hand experience of engaging directly with the authors of proposals again tends to shift attitudes as officials quickly realise the level of commitment and understanding on the part of citizens.

Questions remain about the legitimacy of post-assembly involvement because it tends to become more self-selecting – those with more available time tend to take on the role – and some officials see it as an opportunity to negotiate and bargain with members about the best way to deliver particular policies. In Ireland, organisers do not support post-assembly engagement by members, believing that their role comes to an end when the report is agreed. The appointed Chair of the assembly takes on the role of promoting the assembly recommendations in public and private meetings.

Preparing the Administration

This clash of logics helps explain why the fate of recommendations is perilous. But we do see impacts on policy across assemblies. How is that to be accounted for? Why do we find differences between assemblies when it comes to impact on policy processes?

Quite simply, some commissioners and organisers of assemblies are more prepared than others.

A story I was told emphasises this point well: the first time a public official knew of a climate assembly organised by their administration was when the citizens' report landed on their desk with a number of recommendations suggesting major changes in their area of policy. The official did not react well.

The problem? The lack of consistent follow-up is in large part the result of most practitioners, officials, activists and academics working in the field primarily focusing their attention, energy and resources on designing and implementing the assembly itself. The same level of attention, energy and resources has not been put into designing and implementing follow-up processes.

Part of the explanation is that assemblies are too often organised in haste, with limited preparation time. Under such circumstances, the design and delivery of the assembly takes precedence. For those responsible for organising the assembly, their involvement often ends with the publication of its report.

The contracts of participation organisations are typically only for the design and delivery of the assembly.

The public officials who are responsible for delivering the assembly are not always directly responsible for the policy areas affected by its recommendations.

The governance bodies established to oversee the assembly process are often disbanded when the assembly ends its work.

The follow-up process requires sustained commitment over time. This could be for months or even years after the assembly. The assembly recommendations need to be kept alive as policy windows open and shut. This can be challenging given the cycles of politics, be they issue attention cycles, budget cycles or electoral cycles that can bring in new political actors that were not responsible for setting up the assembly in the first place and may be openly hostile to the process. Ownership of the assembly may not be shared across a public authority which is generally a highly complex and politically divided organisation that works in policy silos with different political and administrative priorities. Public administrations are a complex landing place for recommendations from climate assemblies.

But it is also to do with taste. Practitioners and officials have not chosen to pay enough attention to this critical phase of activity. Engaging citizens is generally more fun than organising the bureaucratic procedures to follow-up the assembly.

While we have a significant knowledge base on how to run assemblies, our understanding of how best to integrate recommendations into commissioning authorities is limited. Lots of advice and guidance exists on how to organise assemblies, but there is almost nothing on how to embed them in the commissioning body. Our collective understanding about how best to prepare public administrations to receive and respond to recommendations is lacking.

For some advocates, only full implementation of the recommendations agreed by assemblies is acceptable. Polish climate assembly practitioner Marcin Gerwin is famous for persuading mayors to implement recommendations that achieve near consensus: 80 per cent or over support from assembly members. But even Gerwin has found that this promise of acceptance does not immediately lead to implementation. Agreed proposals still get stuck in the system.

The most that commissioners of assemblies are generally willing to commit to is that they will seriously consider recommendations. But 'seriously consider' hides a multitude of sins. It is a reasonable democratic expectation that commissioners publicly justify how they have responded to each of the recommendations: whether they are accepted, modified, rejected or still being considered. The concern is that commissioners 'cherry-pick' those recommendations that fit with existing policy and strategy or ideological worldviews.[7]

But justification is not always forthcoming. No wonder, in such circumstances, that assembly members and others committed to the assembly process can become even more politically disillusioned.

A few remits explicitly say something about what is to happen after the assembly reports. The terms of reference for Scotland's Climate Assembly placed an expectation on government that it would formally respond to the assembly's report within six months of receipt. The terms of reference for Irelands' Citizens' Assembly on Biodiversity Loss agreed by both Houses of Parliament clarifies the institutional steps after the assembly delivers its report:

> On receipt, the Houses of the Oireachtas will refer the report of the Assembly for consideration to a relevant Committee of both Houses; the Committee will, in turn, bring its conclusions to the Houses for debate. Furthermore, the Government will provide in the Houses of the Oireachtas a response to each recommendation of the Assembly and, if accepting some or all of the recommendations, will indicate the timeframe it envisages for implementing those recommendations.[8]

Such explicit definition of what is expected after the assembly finishes its work remains relatively unusual. Too often commissioners make general promises that do not always materialise. The most infamous is the 'no filter' promise made by President Macron, not least because it left too much room for interpretation, with some arguing that it was a public promise to implement proposals. Disappointment follows.

Even assemblies that have carefully considered and resourced the follow-up process have not always succeeded in the degree of policy impact expected. Scotland is arguably a case in point.

Follow-Up in Scotland

In many ways the design of the follow-up to Scotland's Climate Assembly was exemplary. The Climate Change Act placed a responsibility on the government to respond within six months to the report of the assembly. The Climate Change Division was given responsibility before the assembly started its work to co-ordinate the government response. The governance bodies – the Secretariat and the Stewarding and Evidence Groups – remained in place to promote the assembly recommendations amongst politicians, public officials and stakeholders. They also provided capacity building and support to assembly members in meetings with politicians and public officials. Following the French practice, the assembly was reconvened to review the government's response. Stakeholders were invited to sign Scotland's Civic Charter on Climate to support the assembly's calls for action.

But these sophisticated structures and processes were not enough. Why?

First, the Covid pandemic delayed the start of the assembly which meant that its recommendations missed the relevant climate policy cycle. Policy windows were no longer open and no dedicated resources were available to integrate assembly recommendations.

Second, while the Climate Change Act specified a government response to the assembly's recommendations within six months, it had nothing to say about what happened afterwards. It did not specify long-term responsibility for action or any further accountability mechanisms. Once the government had made its official response, the team within the Climate Change Division no longer had responsibility to co-ordinate the government's activities. Responsibility now rested with individual policy teams in the areas where the assembly had made recommendations but with no political requirement to report or monitor their actions.

Third, whereas in Ireland the role of parliament is clearly defined, this was not the case in Scotland. Parliament as a whole and the Net Zero Committee in particular were unclear about their own position in the follow-up process.

Finally, two months after the additional assembly weekend reviewing the government's response, the financial year ended. The Secretariat, Stewarding Group and Evidence Group were disbanded.

At that point, no one within the administration had overall responsibility to co-ordinate government action, no dedicated resources were available, and no monitoring processes were in place. Unwittingly, the additional eighth assembly weekend had become a de facto end point to the process.

This does not mean that Scotland's Climate Assembly has had no impact. Its ideas and recommendations continue to reverberate through the political system and civil society. Rather, it is indicative of how even well considered and resourced follow-up plans may not achieve expected outcomes.

Follow-Up in Ireland and Luxembourg

So, what of those nations where impact on policy has been more obviously secured?

The impact of Ireland's first citizens' assembly on climate law is in no small part because of the institutional structures and practices put in place to translate recommendations into the political system. The climate change report of Citizens' Assembly 2016–18 was received by parliament which established a joint parliamentary committee to consider the recommendations. The joint committee's report was submitted to government alongside the assembly's report. The government's response was co-ordinated by the Cabinet Secretary who has the power to ensure action on the part of departments and agencies. The Citizens' Assembly on Biodiversity Loss is following the same process. In Ireland, the importance of tying in parliament oversight and support, and driving the administrative response from the core executive, have been critical to an effective response.

While not integrating parliament into the process, the recommendations of Luxembourg's Climate Citizens' Council were received by the Prime Minister who had publicly commissioned the process. The government response was co-ordinated by his Chief of Staff. Like their counterpart in Ireland, the Chief of Staff and their team ensure that other ministries of state are taking the assembly recommendations seriously. They have the authority of the Prime Minister to demand and, importantly, check action. Luxembourg has gone one step further by regularly updating a publicly accessible Excel sheet with the status of recommendations.

What is striking about Luxembourg is that by the generally agreed standards of citizens' assemblies, it was a bit of a mess. As we discussed in the previous chapter, the assembly lacked transparency, governance arrangements were limited and the organisers had to quickly design an extension to the assembly when it ran out of time and resources. We have the ironic outcome that a not-so-well-designed assembly had a well-designed follow-up that led to impact on policy.

In both Ireland and Luxembourg another factor was at play. The assemblies were timed to contribute to ongoing policy development. In both cases, the governments were preparing climate plans and organised the assemblies to feed directly into that process.

How to ensure that the enabling conditions are in place across electoral, political and administrative bodies to follow up in a way that increases the likelihood of impact on climate governance?

Key success factors for effective follow-up are high-level support, well-considered structures and processes and champions of the assembly who have the licence, skills and capacities to negotiate their way around and across complex commissioning organisations.

- The assembly is timed with relevant policy development work.
- Clarity in the remit as to when and how the commissioner will provide a considered response to each of the recommendations of the assembly.
- Dedicated time and resources and clarity in responsibilities, structures, processes and timelines established *before* the assembly starts its work.
- Responsibility for follow-up located within the core executive, with political leadership giving licence to

---

(Box continued on next page)

(Box continued from previous page)

senior civil servants to drive the process. Parts of the public administration are likely to be resistant to the interventions of a climate assembly. Political support will be necessary to ensure responsiveness.

- Keeping civil servants involved in organising the assembly, along with stakeholder and evidence groups, in place after the assembly has reported to help disseminate the recommendations across the administration and through stakeholder networks.

Two other lessons can be drawn that do not have universal support amongst assembly organisers and advocates:

- Assembly members are generally the best advocates of their recommendations. Capacity building and training is necessary as participation in an assembly does not prepare members to be able to engage with politicians, civil servants and the media. In the same way that civil servants will provide briefings to elected politicians, assembly organisers need to provide support to members.
- External monitoring put in place to oversee the action of public administrations. This can take different forms. For example, reconvening the assembly a few months after the report is received to review government action or a scrutiny or accountability board made up of a selected group of assembly members (ensuring diversity is maintained) and potentially members of the advisory and evidence bodies.

Box 3.2: Lessons for Follow-Up.

Stakeholder Involvement

Remits that restrict assemblies to considering only the role of the state are relatively rare. Ireland's two assemblies asked citizens to deliberate on state action in relation to climate and biodiversity loss. Amsterdam asked the same for its climate action at municipal level. Most remits, though, are more open, which means that some of the recommendations proposed by assemblies will be targeted at stakeholders beyond national government, whether this is some other level or agency of government, private companies, civil society organisations or the general public.

How to ensure that these other stakeholders are motivated and feel some obligation to respond when they did not commission the assembly?

The main strategy to facilitate buy-in is to integrate key stakeholders from the very start of the process in the governance bodies of the assembly and/or for them to act as witnesses, providing evidence when relevant. Stakeholder advisory bodies not only help to ensure balance across different interests, but also tie those who are likely to be affected by recommendations into the process. Eva Saldaña, Director of Greenpeace Spain, has recounted how she was sceptical of assemblies until she took part in the governance body for the national climate assembly. Through direct experience of the deliberations, she became an active champion of the process and its proposals.

The practice that emerged in Scotland, where the stakeholder Stewarding Group remained in place after the report had been delivered, ensured that key actors continued to engage with the assembly process. The Secretariat drew on the networks around these stakeholders to promote the assembly's report and to invite stakeholders beyond the Stewarding Group to sign a Civic Charter in support of the assembly's calls for action.

The German city of Erlangen took the integration of a stakeholder body one step further. Erlangen created a sequenced process involving a local research institute, a stakeholder forum and a citizens' assembly. The role of the institute was initially to scope the range of policies that would be needed for the city to become carbon neutral. These proposals were reviewed by the stakeholder forum and their response was then considered by the assembly. The cycle repeated. Technical experts to stakeholders to citizens. Having gone through this cycle three times, the assembly produced a final set of recommendations. Stakeholders were then invited to sign a City Declaration committing to work towards the agreed goals. Buy-in is arguably more extensive because the stakeholders have had a much more active and creative part to play in the overall process.

The desire to integrate stakeholders more effectively has led to innovation with designs where they engage directly with the randomly selected citizens. This happened in a more informal way in the French Citizens' Convention for the Climate where a number of the proposals were co-constructed with active engagement with stakeholders. Others have formalised these interactions.

In Austria, the members of the Stakeholder Advisory Board of the Citizens' Climate Council were invited to share position papers with the assembly and a dedicated session mid-way through the work programme was designed so that stakeholders and assembly members could exchange ideas. The organisers noticed variations in the level of commitment to the process, with the Chamber of Commerce and the Federation of Austrian Industries less engaged.

The French regional Citizens' Convention for Climate and Biodiversity in Burgundy-Franche-Comté, organised in 2023–4, experimented with bringing stakeholders into the first day of the final two weekends of the assembly at the point where members are developing their recommendations. The first two weekends were members only, as they developed their knowledge and understanding of the climate and ecological crisis and its impact on the region, as well as their confidence and collective agency. Direct involvement of stakeholders recognises their significant knowledge and experience as well as strong interests in co-designing policy proposals. In the end, though, the stakeholders leave the room. As in other assemblies, it is the citizens who make the final decisions.

A more radical approach is taken by G1000 in the Netherlands, not to be confused with the original organisation of the same name in Belgium. G1000 Netherlands aims to create "the system in one room" by using democratic lottery to not only select a large body of everyday people but also stakeholders of different types, including public officials, civic activists and business leaders. While everyday people outnumber the other participants, the protective space for citizens is fundamentally rethought, with citizens and stakeholders working together from the very start of the process. A number of Dutch municipalities have commissioned G1000 assemblies. A comparison between their functionalities and those of more traditional climate assemblies has yet to be undertaken.

It is more difficult to provide robust guidance given that experimentation with different ways of embedding stakeholders within assemblies is still taking place.

- Create opportunities for stakeholders to engage with the assembly process. At minimum, this should be in the form of a stakeholder advisory board. As with public officials, seeing citizens in action can change the perspective of stakeholders, and binding them into the process increases the likelihood that they will respond to recommendations that are within their sphere of responsibility.
- Consider creating opportunities for stakeholders to exchange and collaborate with members in the articulation and design of policy proposals or to provide feedback on draft proposals. Stakeholders bring vital knowledge and experience into the room. Care needs to be taken that they do not dominate assembly members.

Box 3.3: Lessons for Stakeholder Involvement.

Public Communication and Engagement

Climate assemblies involve only a small subset of the wider population. A common criticism is that while members of assemblies have transformative experiences, this does not translate to wider publics. Most people have no idea that the assembly is happening.

How can we ensure that the work and recommendations of assemblies resonate amongst broader publics?

If one of the expectations of assemblies is that they will increase the legitimacy and public acceptance of social action on climate, then the lack of broader public engagement is a problem. The argument here is that wider publics will be more willing to accept low-carbon transitions and adaptations to a warming planet when they know that people like themselves are part of the decision-making process. They may also be more willing to press government to act on assembly recommendations.

Evidence from survey experiments supports this conjecture.[9] When survey respondents are introduced to the idea of a citizens' assembly, we find that controversial policies tend to have broader support when they have been recommended by an assembly compared to other established political institutions. The public seems to have more confidence and trust in the 'everydayness' of assembly members and the process of learning and deliberation they have gone through.

But this is survey evidence. If broader publics do not know when an assembly is happening in the real world, the expectation of public buy-in is in trouble.

It is even more of a problem for those proponents of assemblies who see their value primarily in terms of contributing to public discourse, rather than influencing policy.[10] A precondition is that the public are aware of assemblies.

Media Attention

In France, the Convention was remarkable in the extent to which its recommendations became a widespread topic of public debate. In a 2021 survey, 70 per cent of respondents said they knew about the Convention, with 62 per cent supporting

Figure 3.2: The Austrian Citizens' Climate Assembly © BMK/ Karo Pernegger.

Figure 3.2: Continued.

most of its recommendations.[11] The Austrian Citizens' Climate Assembly also had significant public recognition and support.

The recent Citizens' Assembly on Biodiversity Loss in Ireland has generated a high level of media interest and raised the salience of the nature crisis amongst politicians and the public. Media and public interest is likely to increase when the government makes its response.

Media attention on the other national assemblies has been more modest – and for advocates, frankly disappointing. Why is this?

Most have found it difficult to attract media attention, whether traditional or new media. As such they have not resonated with broader publics. Some of this can be put down to poor strategy and/or poor resourcing. Most assemblies rely heavily on ensuring transparency through an official website where the different elements of the lifecycle of the assembly are laid out: the recruitment process, streaming of the evidence provided to members, governance structures, etc. But this is not enough to attract and sustain media interest.

The lack of familiarity with assemblies amongst journalists is a major stumbling block. The media needs to be courted and educated. The news value of assemblies is not immediately obvious to journalists for whom political conflict and polarisation are defining features of their analysis of democracy. The different elements of the lifecycle of an assembly need to be actively 'sold'.

This is precisely what the French and the Austrians aimed to achieve with their media strategies, both of which were well-resourced. Both spent around €1 million – just under 10 per cent of the budget in France; around half in Austria – dwarfing the resources available to most other assemblies. In Austria and France, organisers actively educated journalists about the different stages of the process, from recruitment through to government response. And both made members available for interview and engaged with social media influencers to extend their reach. The opportunity to personalise assemblies through stories of members proved particularly attractive, especially for regional and local media outlets.

Austria also employed two civil society engagement officers who were able to lead more in-depth communication with interested parties such as regional government climate and energy managers, climate NGOs and activists. They distributed a newsletter after every session of the assembly and continued their work raising the profile of the assembly after it had reported.

In terms of media interest, the French Convention had the advantage that it took place against the backdrop of significant social unrest and a weakened President who publicly associated himself with the process and appeared to have promised to implement the proposals. That has news value. While assembly members in both France and Austria organised themselves into a civic organisation once they had delivered their reports, Les 150 in France gained much more media attention, again because of the way that the assembly had become part of public and political discourse. The failure in Austria by the government to respond formally to the assembly was reported but the debate was not as politically febrile as in France.

Political context can be critical. The Polish Citizens' Assembly on Energy Costs enjoyed reasonably high media interest given its relatively meagre communications budget. In large part this is because it gained support from the main opposition party and the topic of the assembly gained salience with the Russian invasion of Ukraine and its effect on energy prices.

Ireland is the other example where media attention on assemblies is high. The institutionalisation of assemblies has changed media attitudes. They happen fairly regularly and are taken seriously by parliament and government. The significant political and constitutional impact of the recommendations on same sex marriage and abortion were a game changer for ensuring media interest.

The climate recommendations of the Irish Citizens' Assembly 2016–18 did not register with the media because they were crowded out by the debate about the assembly's abortion recommendations. In comparison, the Biodiversity Loss assembly received significant media coverage during its work, with a respected RTÉ journalist attending regularly and publishing relevant stories. Two TikTok influencers were invited to the launch and to follow the process to try to broaden the audience. While the Irish are more protective of their members, organisers still exploit the local and regional connections of assembly members. The independent Chair also plays an active role through media interviews and public appearances at major events – for example, the Chair of the Biodiversity Loss assembly met with the largest farming organisations at the national ploughing championships, Europe's largest outdoor event.

Public Engagement

Communication tends to be one way, with organisers and advocates attempting to get the message about an assembly out to the public via established and new media. For some assemblies, public engagement has meant more than just one-way communication. The ambition has been to create a more proactive interaction between wider publics and the assembly before, during and after the assembly. As with stakeholder engagement, this work remains fairly experimental.

Before the assembly begins its work, the ambition of a small number of assemblies has been to involve the public in agenda-setting: clarifying some aspect of the remit of the assembly. The organisers of the Spanish Citizens' Assembly for the Climate created an online survey which enabled 1,500 submissions on potential themes to be addressed by the assembly. In Poland, 45 local civic events of different scale and structure were organised that engaged around 700 people, with their ideas feeding into the framing of the nationwide assembly on energy costs.

The most impressive pre-assembly engagement is arguably the National Conversation that took place before the People's Assembly for Nature in the UK. Over a four-week period, organisers received 30,000 submissions on people's relationship with nature and how it could be protected. Thoughts and ideas were shared online and at 74 events across the UK, including Future Arts Centres, National Trust properties, schools and football clubs. These were presented in creative formats to members of the People's Assembly to help inform their deliberations.[12]

A similarly sophisticated pre-assembly engagement exercise took place in Devon – a mainly rural county in the southwest of England.[13] In 2019, Devon County Council convened a partnership of 27 organisations – the Devon Climate Emergency Response Group (DCERG) – to create a Carbon Plan. The first two steps of the process were expert hearings on a range of themes followed by a public call for evidence from anyone living or working in Devon. The third step was the climate assembly. The DCERG narrowed the assembly's remit down to three policy challenges that had consistently emerged from the stakeholder and public engagement exercises: renewable energy, car use and the retrofit of buildings.

Many assemblies invite public submissions while they are undertaking their work, typically through an online platform. These tend to be one way, with assembly members receiving input from those outside the process. For example, the French Convention received around 3,400 submissions.

No climate assembly has attempted to replicate the more dialogical approach taken by the original British Columbia Citizens' Assembly on Electoral Reform. During this process, members were supported to organise local community meetings where they took evidence directly from members of the public and local organised interest groups. Like most public meetings they tended to attract those who were already politically engaged, with strong views on the subject.

Austria stands alone with its digital experimentation with Pol.is – an argument mapping platform. Pol.is has distinctive features. It allows participants to vote on statements (agree, disagree, unsure) and to add their own statements for review by others. Based on this engagement, the platform provides insights into where broad consensus and dissensus can be found on the statements. Pol.is was designed by the social movement vTaiwan and has been adopted more widely for public engagement exercises by governments. But it had not been used in conjunction with a citizens' assembly before.

Midway through the assembly process, Pol.is was seeded with 200 statements from across the five workstreams based on emerging ideas from the members. Over 5,000 people participated by voting on the assembly's ideas and/or submitting their own statements. Over 5,700 statements were submitted and around 833,000 votes were registered. This not only showed areas of public support for assembly ideas, but exposed areas of public contention, such as vegetarian/vegan diets, food afford-ability and road pricing.

The Global Assembly took a different approach. Rather than ena-bling public engagement to feed into the assembly, organisers used the Global Assembly as an opportunity to seed community assem-blies across the world. Anyone who was interested could download a step-by-step guide on how to run a community assembly, includ-ing recruiting a diverse group of participants, activities to explore the climate and ecological crisis, facilitating deep conversations and decision making. Organisers have limited data on how their resources were used, but they know that more than 370 people reg-istered to run an assembly across at least 41 countries.[14]

Whether using rather old-fashioned public submissions or more sophisticated Pol.is data, the challenge faced by organisers and assembly members is always how to integrate this input.

First, how and in what format to present the massive amount of data to assembly members without overwhelming them? After all, they are already having to process the extensive input from witnesses. In Ireland, for example, submissions are randomly allocated to different tables.

Second, what value to place on this data? Engagement is likely to be from more politically engaged citizens and interest groups. Given the effort that assembly organisers place on ensuring a diverse body of members and balanced evidence in deliberations, it is difficult to figure out how best to manage and integrate less balanced input from wider publics during the process. We should expect further experimentation here.

Irish assemblies lead the way in post-assembly public engage-ment through constitutional referendums, but as yet, these haven't taken place on climate or ecological issues. Following assemblies, the government has organised referendums on same-sex marriage, abortion, age restrictions for the presidency and gender equality. In all cases, this is because the recommendations of the relevant assembly included one or more constitutional ammendments, which under Irish law require a referendum to be implemented. The Biodiversity Loss assembly has recommended four constitutional changes to substantive and procedural rights for humans and nonhuman nature. Whether the government will agree to put one or more of these to a referendum is yet to be seen.

In France, the assembly's remit enabled members to propose referendums, alongside laws and regulations. Three out of the 149 proposals were for referendums, all of which were blocked by the President or Parliament.

Some advocates of climate assemblies have proposed that recommendations be put directly to a public vote as a way of bypassing political institutions. A recent proposal from the author and activist David van Reybrouck is that this should be done via 'preferendum', where voters are able to indicate the extent of their support for propositions rather than a crude yes or no.[15] Regardless of the merits of linking assemblies with referendums, it is unclear quite how the large number of proposals that emerge from climate assemblies could be put to a public vote in a way that ensures reasonable levels of understanding and debate across wider publics.

Organisers and advocates are still trying to figure out how best to interest the media in climate assemblies and to engage the wider public in their work. Some lessons can be drawn from current practice.

(Box continued on next page)

(Box continued from previous page)

- Organisers and advocates need to develop media and communication strategies that are sensitive to the different elements of assemblies – recruitment, evidence, deliberation, recommendations, follow-up, etc. Different approaches may be needed at different points in the assembly lifecycle.
- A balance needs to be struck between media access and protection of members and their deliberations. Training needs to be given to those members who are interested in engaging with the media.
- Active outreach and capacity building is often needed to engage journalists and social media influencers who will generally be unfamiliar with assemblies.
- Personal stories of members are particularly attractive to the media – as are recommendations in areas of social contestation (e.g., diet and mobility). The latter may be frustrating to organisers, but it is impossible to control.
- The potential to organise public engagement around assemblies has generally been underexploited. This can be both an opportunity to feed ideas into the assembly from outside – from setting the remit to feedback on draft recommendations – and to seed community conversations using material from the assembly.
- Careful consideration needs to be given about how and in what format the input from wider publics is to be integrated into the assembly's work.

Box 3.4: Lessons for Public Communication and Engagement.

Where Next for Climate Assemblies?

When you're in the middle of the action, it is difficult to get the distance necessary to make sound judgements about future trends. But let's give it a go.

It is less than five years since the French Convention began its work. But we are now in a different place. At least 200 climate assemblies of varying quality have been organised in the intervening period. We have learned a lot about what works and what does not. Thanks to intiatives like the Knowledge Network on Climate Assemblies (KNOCA), those commissioning, designing and organising assemblies are in a much better place to implement processes that impact climate governance and broader public debate. We are well aware of the importance of getting the remit, follow-up, communication and public and stakeholder engagement right.

Much of what has happened over the last five years is based on modifications to the standard operating model – i.e., assemblies commissioned by government that last a defined period of time before delivering a report and recommendations.

This standard operating model of climate assemblies is likely to remain the most common practice for the time being. The question is what happens next. Can assemblies become a more central part of climate governance in a way that helps us address the climate and ecological crisis more effectively?

Having seen waves of other forms of participation, we have reason to be worried. Participatory budgeting (PB) in the late 1990s and early 2000s is a salutary lesson for democratic innovation. PB is a form of citizen participation in which citizens are given direct control over the allocation of parts of the municipal budget. Originating in the Brazilian city of Porto Alegre, PB spread across Brazil, Latin America and then across other continents. Everyone wanted to be part of the wave. It has been estimated that over 7,000 PBs have taken place across the world. The original Brazilian model rested on significant state restructuring to deliver impressive social justice outcomes. But with diffusion came the watering down of the radical edge. Later PBs were a shadow of the earlier democratic innovation.[1] PB lost its lustre. Its rise was followed by a plateau of less impactful practice and then a decline in activity as people looked for the next big thing. We still find niches where PB remains vibrant, but not the global movement of democratic and social change that many had hoped for. Is this to be the fate of climate assemblies?

That is one possible future. An alternative sees a second wave of climate assemblies that is qualitatively different from the first and which deepens the democratic and transformative character of climate governance. At least four intriguing developments are likely to shape this future.

The first is a shift from one-off assemblies to permanent bodies. The second, climate assemblies organised by civil society independent from and at times challenging the state. Third, the embedding of systems thinking within assemblies in recognition of the systematic nature of the crises we are facing. And finally, a dynamic movement for assemblies that reaches from public officials to radical social movement activists.

Some of these developments point in different directions, so the trajectory of the next wave of assemblies is far from clearcut. Again, these reflections focus on the experience of assemblies in Europe. How well they travel to other parts of the world is unclear.

Permanent Assemblies

In 2022, Brussels and Milan city administrations broke the mould.[2] The standard operating model of one-off assemblies was replaced with bodies that were intended to be new permanent features of municipal climate governance. The two assemblies work in different ways, but the principle is the same: a regular annual cycle feeds citizens' recommendations into decision making in the city. The two cities have built on the ground-breaking permanent assemblies in the East Belgium region and Paris. These first two assemblies work on any policy issue that citizens find relevant. In the case of Brussels and Milan, the assemblies' remits are focused on climate.

The first one hundred members of the Brussels Capital-Region climate assembly were selected by democratic lottery in late 2022. They worked together between February and April 2023 and submitted recommendations to the government in June 2023. The government provided initial feedback in September 2023 and a more detailed explanation of its actions is required within a year. So far so similar to the standard operating model. The difference? In 2024, the cycle began again with a new set of Brussels residents drawn by lot. Figure 4.1 summaries the basic structure of the permanent assembly.

The first cycle worked on an agenda set by the municipal government. It focused on housing, renovation and greening the city. The remits of future cycles will be set by a group of 25 members of the previous assembly – the agenda committee – after consulting with the government, political parties and other stakeholders. Having experienced a remit with three separate issues, the citizens decided that the second cycle of the assembly would deal with a single issue. They chose food and nutrition having been advised that it would be timely for policy development in this area as the government was about to prepare a revision to its current policy and programmes.

Another neat innovation of the Brussels assembly that could be taken up by standard one-off assemblies is the creation of a follow-up committee made up of ten members of that year's assembly to oversee government action on their recommendations. They have the right to meet with ministers at least twice and can ask to meet anyone from the administration or cabinet to be informed about government activities.

The Milan permanent assembly also works on an annual cycle. The main difference with Brussels is that its focus is on the implementation of the municipal Air and Climate Plan that is in place until at least 2030. The Plan aims to reduce greenhouse gas emissions, improve air quality and combat the effects of climate change. The assembly considers how existing policies within the

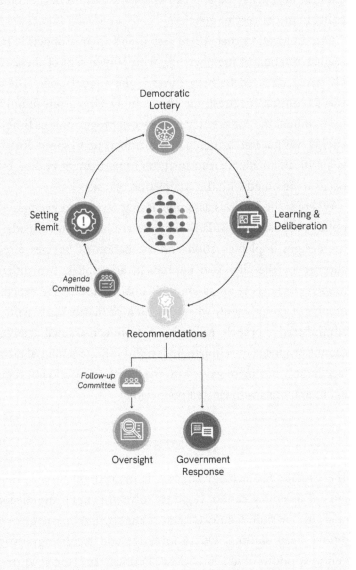

Figure 4.1: The Brussels Permanent Climate Assembly © European Climate Foundation.

plan are best delivered and can assess the actions of the municipality in its delivery of policies.

One innovation that Milan tested and then dropped is more regular rotation of membership, with 50 per cent of the assembly being replaced halfway through the annual cycle. The aim was to constantly refresh the citizen body. Organisers found this undermined the consistency of the work programme as time and energy was put into bringing new members up to speed. Rotation is a critical complement to sortition in permanent bodies, but it needs to be timed with the completion of tasks.

Whereas the Brussels assembly is empowered to generate new policy proposals, in Milan members are limited to considering the design, implementation and evaluation of policies already adopted by the city. Two permanent assemblies; two different models. Brussels is an assembly primarily tied to the executive branch of government, whereas Milan primarily deals with the administrative branch. Milan has a more constrained agenda. It cannot propose new climate policy. But it has a potential advantage in only having to work with the bureaucracy and not requiring interactions with elected politicians.

Why Permanency?

The climate and ecological crisis is in constant flux. A single, one-off assembly cannot hope to 'solve' this multi-dimensional crisis in one shot. Contexts keep changing. Environmental conditions keep shifting. Our knowledge and technology evolve. Policy windows open and close. Political and social attitudes adapt. Mitigation and adaptation strategies require constant policy adjustments, and new and increasingly complex challenges emerge. We need a participatory structure that can be responsive to those shifts.

A permanent structure has other advantages. As discussed earlier, political and bureaucratic actors can be resistant to assemblies. They are unfamiliar and often sceptical of this way of doing politics. A permanent body enables public authorities and other stakeholders to adapt their working practices to citizen input. Over time, culture change and embedding is more likely. Recommendations are more likely to have a favourable reception. And a more permanent structure can improve oversight and monitoring of action on recommendations.

Permanency enables learning from each cycle. Assuming room for reflexivity and innovation, the working practices of permanent assemblies and the structures and practices of the commissioning authority can be refined over time.

Permanency also promises broader social impact. Knowledge and understanding of climate assemblies will increase as more citizens receive invitations and participate in the process – or at least know someone who has. The more people are aware of and directly experience assemblies, the larger the potential transformative effect. The hope too is that permanency can build public trust and legitimacy in this more democratic form of climate governance – assuming the commissioner and other stakeholders are responsive to the assembly. A permanent assembly promises to be a counterpower within climate governance against established economic, social and political interests and electoral dynamics that are a break on transformation.

We have seen some of these impacts in Ireland. However, permanency distinguishes Brussels and Milan from what is happening there. Citizens' assemblies have been institutionalised and embedded in Ireland: the national government has commissioned six since 2013, with a commitment from political parties to run more in the future. But the number of future assemblies and their remits rests with the political class. While the first assembly dealt with climate and a more recent one has examined biodiversity loss, it is not at all clear if these topics will be returned to in future. Brussels and Milan ensure that climate is continually considered.

But permanent assemblies can have limitations. Sceptics worry that they may prove nothing more than an elaborate and expensive example of citizen-washing – engaging citizens to simply legitimise existing government (in)activity. The hope is that where power lies with citizens to set the agenda and to monitor government action, citizen-washing is less likely.

While both the Brussels and Milan assemblies are codified – they have legal or regulatory status – that does not mean that they will be taken seriously. Codification alone does not ensure participation is embedded within climate governance. Permanent bodies need resourcing. A number of high-profile participatory processes – from the celebrated participatory budgeting in Porto Alegre in Brazil to the innovative and experimental NHS Citizen in the UK – suffered slow deaths from under-resourcing and de-prioritisation.[3] If these permanent assemblies are to be successful in the long run, they need to build and sustain political and public commitment and support.

Brussels and Milan are first movers. Other European cities and regions have started permanent processes (Rouen) and are in the planning stages (Catalonia, Copenhagen). What future models for permanent climate assemblies will emerge is an open question. The assemblies in Brussels and Milan have already established an interesting array of powers: the empowerment of selected residents in Brussels to set the agenda and to engage in meaningful oversight of government action on their recommendations; and the capacity of members in Milan to scrutinise government implementation of its municipal climate plan. These are all intriguing developments.

Where permanent bodies prove their worth, we might reasonably imagine extensions of their powers. This might include the practice developed initially in a few Polish municipalities where assemblies are given decision making rights. Where there is near consensus amongst members, the commissioning body has a duty to implement.

But we should not understand empowerment as simply full decision-making power or nothing. A more nuanced range of powers might include the power to review government proposals and to delay actions where the assembly believes policy runs against meaningful climate action. Or for the assembly to propose policy developments which require a supermajority of elected chambers to halt. Or the right of the assembly to send one or more of its proposals to referendum (or preferendum).

Innovation in permanent assembly practice may take a number of different directions.

Assemblies Beyond the State

The mental model of success that most advocates of assemblies hold is governments commissioning and responding to regular assemblies, with the embedding of permanent assemblies by government as the ideal. Challenging that assumption is a number of climate assemblies organised by non-state organisations and actors, such as civil society organisations and academic research-ers. Four of the national assemblies to date have been organised in this way, a small number at sub-national levels and one at trans-national level.[4]

A number of these initiatives have been demonstration projects aimed at persuading government to take up the mantle and com-mission assemblies themselves. Or they have been organised by researchers with the primary intention of analysing the delibera-tive qualities of these participatory spaces. These demonstration and research projects are often the least interesting examples.

Way more interesting are those assemblies that have been organ-ised explicitly to challenge inaction on the part of government and other societal actors.

The German Citizens' Assembly for Climate, for example, was organised by the civil society organisations BürgerBegehren Kli-maschutz (Citizens' Climate Protection Initiative) and Scientists for Future. Their primary aim was for the assembly to raise the profile of climate policy amongst political parties during the fed-eral election and the coalition negotiations and policy develop-ment that followed.

A number of citizens' assemblies – including on aspects of climate policy – have been run independently across Central and Eastern Europe. The national Polish Citizens' Assembly on Energy Costs was organised by the Shipyard Foundation[5] and the Climate Assembly in Skopje on endemic air pollution in the city was organised by the Zip Institute. In these cases, the assemblies were organised by respected civil society organisations to dem-onstrate robust democratic practice in explicit contrast to widely distrusted public authorities. Their end goal is for assemblies to be part of the rebuilding of democratic climate governance.

The People's Assembly on Nature was commissioned by three respected conservation organisations in the UK: the Royal Society for the Protection of Birds (RSPB), the World Wide Fund for Nature (WWF) and the National Trust. These are mainstream civil society organisations that have embraced this deliberative democratic method in recognition of the limitations of their existing advocacy and campaigning strategies. The assembly created the People's Plan for Nature that set out 26 calls for action targeted at national governments, local governments, businesses, charities and NGOs, individuals and communities.

For the three commissioning bodies, the Plan is a different type of intervention into the politics of nature. It is not the voice of professional advocates or activists, but rather the considered judgements of a diverse group of ordinary, everyday citizens. It does not necessarily line up with all of their priorities, but the commissioners and other nature NGOs are integrating the assembly's vision and calls for action into their policy advocacy and campaigning activities. It may well be a new model of the use of citizens' assemblies. Similar to the German assembly, the endgame is for civil society organisations to commission these processes as a way of opening up and altering the dynamics of political space.

The Swedish Climate Assembly has been organised by a consortium of researchers led by the Stockholm Resilience Centre, an international research centre on resilience and sustainability science. Unlike other purely academic projects, the organisers have the explicit aim for the assembly to contribute to public and political discourse on Sweden's commitment to and action on the Paris Agreement in a context of perceived government backsliding.

Figure 4.2: UK – People's Assembly on Nature © Jemima Stubbs/ www.involve.org.uk.

Figure 4.2: Continued.

At the time of writing, the assembly has only just begun its work, so it is unclear how the strategy will unfold.

A proposed national assembly in Norway has similar aims of catalysing public debate and action. In this case, the target is Norway's growing oil and gas wealth in times of climate and ecological crisis. The main political parties are committed to continue fossil fuel extraction and are not questioning the profits of the sovereign wealth fund which have increased significantly because of the war in Ukraine. It is these profits of extraction that resource the generous pensions and welfare state enjoyed by Norwegians. For a coalition of humanitarian and other civil society organisations, brought together by the not-for-profit organisation SoCentral, these contradictions need to be the subject of public and political debate. Hence a climate assembly organised independently of the state.

We are also seeing the emergence of assemblies taking place *within* organisations to consider the implications of climate for their operations. One example is the Assembly of the Transition. organised at the University of Lausanne in Switzerland, that brings together academic and administrative staff and students selected by lottery. It aims to reflect the diversity of the university community in focusing action on 'the overall goal of bringing its impacts within planetary boundaries while ensuring the basic needs and well-being of all.'[6] I am aware of activists within the aviation industry in the UK working towards a climate assembly for workers to consider how it can transition in the face of the climate and ecological crisis.

These civil society and other non-state commissioned assemblies can be understood as explicit countervailing powers against inaction by government and other social and economic institutions.

They explicitly challenge the status quo in different ways, but do not eschew the political system as a whole.

A more radical position within social movements is discernible, one that more explicitly challenges the system. Roger Hallam, founder of Extinction Rebellion (XR) and the Humanity Project, goes as far as to argue that citizens' assemblies could be a 'revolutionary confrontation with the carbon state'.[7] The logic here is that if government is dysfunctional and captured by entrenched interests, then we should not be surprised when assemblies (even those commissioned by civil society organisations) have relatively little impact. Better to create assemblies independent of the state that can act as a different sort of countervailing power against government and corporate interests. A power that challenges the very logic and legitimacy of our governing institutions and carbon-based economy. In this scenario, climate assemblies become explicitly more political. The state cannot and will not provide the political space to challenge the current system and its logics. Climate assemblies are vanguards of a more authentic democratic governance to come.

For some of its organisers and advocates, the Global Assembly can be thought of in these more oppositional terms. The assembly was explicitly organised independently of any of the existing institutions of global governance and national governments. Debate rages as to whether future iterations of the Global Assembly should maintain this independence or whether it should dock with particular institutions. Radical and more mainstream interpretations of its future co-exist.

Organisation by non-state actors offers different potential trajectories for climate assemblies in which creating these independent deliberative spaces is a much more political act, often as a form of direct contestation with and against state power. In so doing, it raises a distinct set of challenges about how to establish robust governance and set remits in this context and how to communicate with and engage broader publics. How can civil society organisations ensure integrity in the design and delivery of climate assemblies such that assemblies are recognised as legitimate? How can pathways to impact be defined and realised when the state is not commissioning the assembly or willingly receiving its recommendations?

This is uncomfortable territory for some within the citizens' assembly community of practice who see their role as supplementing liberal democratic politics – definitely not in confrontational or oppositional terms. For others, it is the cutting edge of practice and the vanguard for a revitalised democratic politics to address our planetary crisis.

Systems Thinking

The Intergovernmental Panel on Climate Change (IPCC) and the Intergovernmental Science-Policy Platform on Biodiversity and Ecosystem Services (IPBES) are clear that systems change is necessary to respond to the climate and ecological crisis. For the IPCC, 'Limiting global warming to 1.5 degrees Celsius would require rapid, far-reaching and unprecedented changes in all aspects of society.'[8] Similarly, the IPBES states: 'Goals for conserving and sustainably using nature and achieving sustainability cannot be met by current trajectories, and goals for 2030 and beyond may only be achieved through transformative changes across economic, social, political and technological factors.'[9]

A deep and troubling critique of climate assemblies as currently organised is that they fail to take the systemic nature of the climate and ecological crisis seriously enough. Assemblies generate vision statements and a range of recommendations for action that go well beyond current commitments of most governments and political parties. But do they go far enough?

The concern is that assemblies are generally not framed or structured to support systems thinking: that is, to comprehensively analyse interactions between policy domains, the externalities of policies (e.g., the impact of supply chains on vulnerable geographies) or the structural causes of the climate and ecological crisis and the types of transformations that may be needed to respond effectively. Rather assemblies tend to focus on and produce recommendations across a number of different policy areas without necessarily considering these broader dynamics.

It is not that citizens cannot think systematically or are not willing to consider systems change. We can find reference to elements of systems change within assembly reports. For example, Scotland's Climate Assembly challenged the focus on economic growth and GDP. A recommendation from the Spanish Climate Assembly makes the case for enhancing information on degrowth. But these ideas are not developed in detail and most of the reports are focused on specific areas of policy.

An analysis of the recommendations of the French Convention by the think tank IDDRI suggests that many of them had transformative implications:

> The scope of what is proposed incorporates a large number of components (social justice, innovation, advertising, education, trade policy, circular economy, etc.) and indicates willingness to refocus every dimension of

our society on the climate priority. It shows the need to radically transform our entire economic system and our lifestyles.[10]

But Claire Mellier, one of the initiators of the Global Assembly and Stuart Capstick, an environmental social scientist, contend that systems thinking is constrained by the way that most assemblies are broken into workstreams focused on particular policy areas. When members in the French Convention raised issues about the nature of growth, GDP and the impact of the profit motive as blockages to the transition in the first weekend session, this did not fit with the more policy-centric approach defined by the Governance Committee. As Mellier and Capstick argue:

> Despite the fact that the Convention's process was shaped by citizens much more than other climate citizens' assemblies, the process still did not allow, for example, discussion about the political economy and critical societal indicators such as GDP in connection with alternative models of development, oil and gas subsidies, the financial system, or the leverage that banks or pensions schemes have in the climate and ecological crisis.[11]

As the political scientist David Kahane contends, 'if you believe that climate change is a symptom of deeper pathologies in social, economic, and political systems that require deep transformation or revolution', then we need to rethink how assemblies are framed and structured to enable systems thinking.[12]

Why is this not done? Kahane believes that it is down to a combination of the pressure of time to organise assemblies, the lack of ready-to-hand language and tools and the strength of underlying assumptions amongst the community of deliberative practice that tends to privilege more reformist, piecemeal approaches to change. It is hard to disrupt our established ways of doing things – including the way we organise deliberative processes.

We can add an additional explanation. It is hard to imagine many governments being willing to commission assemblies that are framed to consider widespread transformative change – even if it is precisely that sort of change the IPCC, IPBES and other established scientific bodies are recommending. When governments are so implicated in current economic and social systems, will they sanction assemblies where our current growth model, climate injustices and colonial implications of the climate and ecological crisis are front and centre?

This may well be where civil society-led assemblies have an advantage in their capacity to experiment and create democratic spaces where more structural and systemic questions are raised. We can see elements of this, for example, in the way that the Norwegian assembly proposes to bring into question the contradictions of the country's growing oil and gas wealth. But it's not easy to do. Even the Global Assembly was criticised for taking too much of an 'eco-modernist' approach which did not give space for alternative worldviews.[13]

What might more systems-focused assemblies look like? We can answer this in at least two ways: the integration of tools and techniques to promote systems thinking; and the extension of the constituency of the assembly.

Systems Tools and Techniques

Distinct fields of systems modelling, scenario planning and systemic design exist that could inform the design and delivery of climate assemblies. But the connections between these fields and those working on citizens' assemblies are tenuous. Our experience in KNOCA of trying to bring these worlds together has been challenging given the different languages the communities use. It is noticeable, for example, that when scenario planners talk of public participation, they tend to be thinking of stakeholder engagement. They primarily work with organisations and institutions with specialist knowledge and resources to shape the system. Citizens' assemblies are very different participatory spaces.

Experimentation is happening. For each of Climate Assembly UK's workstreams, the Expert Leads presented three scenarios. Members were able to consider and vote on policies within those scenarios and between the scenarios themselves. These included transformational proposals within the policy streams, although deliberations on broader cross-cutting structural questions were not facilitated.

Scotland's Climate Assembly used scenarios and storytelling to extend members' imagination through four fictional stories of a day in the life of a person living in Scotland in 2040, developed in collaboration with the international sustainability organisation, Forum for the Future.[14] The four stories were used as the basis for small group work exploring potential barriers and opportunities for change at different levels – individuals, households, organisations.

The organisers of Grenoble's Citizens' Convention for the Climate used the reference pathways for carbon neutrality published by the French Agency for Ecological Transition to develop territory-specific scenarios. These informed members' vision for the region and the development of recommendations in an iterative movement between scenarios, vision and proposals.

The organisers of the Swedish Climate Assembly include specialists in systems modelling. Over a number of months in preparation for the assembly, they considered how to integrate different approaches to modelling. Models that interrogate how systems are connected. Models that emphasise system dynamics such as feedbacks, time lags, stocks and flows. Models that focus on indirect drivers and barriers to change, be they events, patterns, trends, underlying structures and mental models.[15] Their concern, though, is that such models could overwhelm members of assemblies, giving undue status to a range of hidden judgements and assumptions. They became much more attracted to bottom-up participatory approaches that can increase citizens' agency by helping them to understand the interconnected nature of the climate and ecological crisis, craft their own collective models and interrogate structural drivers. Recognising and wrestling with the potential tensions between modelling and deliberation is itself a first step. The next will be further experimentation.

Mellier and Capstick are also less inclined to go down the more formal modelling route, instead arguing that systemic design has a large toolkit of methods that can help organisers craft and run processes that 'are more attentive to complex, interacting dynamics.'[16] Their preferred approach is to combine an introduction to critical and systems thinking, sessions that bring different perspectives to bear on the political economy of climate change and alternative economic models, and an acknowledgment of different worldviews on the climate and ecological crisis. They are particularly exercised about the need to build the capacity of members (and practitioners) to be able to explore the different ways that power is exercised in society – and the assembly itself.

Expanding the Constituency of Assemblies

A second approach to transformative thinking is to consider who is in the room. A hard-won lesson from feminist and racial justice activists is that if key parts of the social system are not present, then their interests are unlikely to be considered. What might this mean for assemblies?

In the last chapter, we mentioned the practice developed by G1000 Netherlands of bringing 'the system in one room' by mixing randomly selected citizens with actors from political, social and cultural institutions and organisations. While this more accurately reflects the broader social system, whether it is more likely to encourage transformative thinking is an open question.

One way of bringing the impact of the current system to the fore is to ensure that those most vulnerable to the climate and ecological crisis are present amongst the members of the assembly. Work by feminist scholars has made it clear just how important it is for women and minority groups to be present in a critical mass in political spaces. The tendency of assembly organisers to ensure the inclusion of one or two indigenous peoples, for example, is often not much more than tokenism.

A common response is to argue that it is enough for the assembly to hear stories directly from witnesses from vulnerable social groups. The organisers of the early Irish assemblies often speak of the way that hearing directly from children of same sex partners and from those who experienced a lack of access to abortion services shifted preconceptions.

But this only gets us so far. We need to ensure that the experience of being vulnerable to the climate and ecological crisis has a distinct presence within the deliberating body and is not just another piece of evidence. This may require substantially oversampling particular social groups. This is anathema to many advocates of assemblies for whom the strong resemblance between the characteristics of the assembly and the broader population is fundamental for its legitimacy. It raises the question of whether public identification with an assembly is undermined if we engage in affirmative action, where some groups are over-represented in recognition of their vulnerabilities. Concerns about climate and ecological justice and seeking to right historical wrongs may well clash with concerns about perceived legitimacy.

Even more contentious is the argument that systems thinking requires us to directly involve non-compatriots: people living outside the political jurisdiction of the assembly but affected by the decisions that will be made. The case of those living in areas of the Global South despoiled by mining of rare metals that fuel the green transition in Europe is an obvious example. What status should peoples from these impacted communities have in climate assemblies in Europe? This is a classic problem for democratic theory. The principle that all those affected by a decision should be included makes sense philosophically. However, politically it is hard to imagine a public authority sanctioning membership of an assembly for non-residents.

The long-term impacts of climate policy bring into question the status of future generations within assemblies. After all, they will suffer more of the direct impacts of a warming world. One approach is to directly involve young people. The Youth Climate Assembly in the Idra-Viru region of Estonia, for example, brought together 33 randomly selected young people between 16–29 years of age to influence the future of a region that has relied heavily on the economic contribution of oil shale mining and burning.

More recent experimentation has involved even younger children. The Children and Young People's Assembly on Biodiversity Loss, involving members aged 7–17, ran in parallel and fed its recommendations into the adult process. Scotland's Climate

Assembly ran a process engaging school children. The designer of these processes, Katie Reid, has made the case for exploring intergenerational dialogue within a single assembly rather than separate assemblies and processes.[17]

Engaging children and young people gets us so far. But what about unborn generations, particularly those more distant? Assembly and assembly-like processes are experimenting with how the interests of future generations might be incorporated.[18] Missions Publiques, the French participation organisation, is incorporating the seventh-generation principle as a way of decentring the interests of current generations with noticeable effects on the orientation of members. Future Design, a process developed by the Japanese economist Tatsuyoshi Saijo, asks participants to consider proposals as if they were living 50 to 100 years in the future. To give them a sense of the importance of the task, organisers ask them to dress in ceremonial robes as part of the process.

A category of inclusion that pushes the design and practice of assemblies even further is nonhuman nature. An increasingly common approach is to leave the confines of the assembly room and spend time in those spaces and places that could be deeply affected by decisions. The Irish Citizens' Assembly on Biodiversity Loss included field trips to different ecologically sensitive sites to give members first-hand experience of what they were deliberating about. For many, it was their first time in such environments. The Children and Young People's Assembly that ran in parallel undertook some of its work outside in more natural surroundings. Other more creative approaches ask members to take on the role of different nonhuman entities and even ecosystems so that members can consider how they will be affected by any decision, often through forms of guided meditation. Such techniques are at the leading edge of assembly practice – and, not surprisingly, are for some controversial and one step too far.

Systems thinking is a huge challenge for the commissioning, design, implementation and evaluation of climate assemblies – and for thinking about what meaningful impact means. How far can assemblies integrate systems and scenario modelling? How far can they expand the constituency of assemblies? How much transformational work can we expect assemblies to do – and with what effect?

It is an open question as to whether these challenges will encourage a new generation of climate assembly practice or put too much pressure on assemblies and break the model.

Building a Movement

Climate assemblies have an intriguing range of advocates. From elected and appointed officials through to activists within radical social movements. From practitioners designing and delivering assemblies to academics. From those looking to improve the efficiency and effectiveness of climate governance to those who see assemblies as a building block for a new democratic politics that will enable us to collectively face the worsening climate and ecological crisis.

The diversity of this growing movement for climate assemblies is unusual for a relatively new, niche institution. As with assemblies themselves, diversity is a strength but also throws up challenges.

Chances are many people have come across the idea of citizens' assemblies through the activism of social movements such as XR. One of the core demands of XR is for governments to establish an empowered citizens' assembly on climate and ecological justice.[19] I must admit to being rather surprised during XR's uprising in Autumn 2019 to discover that Whitehall – the main road running from Trafalgar Square to Parliament in London – was occupied for days by activists with banners and slogans declaring 'Citizens' Assemblies Now'. As XR spread across the globe, so too did knowledge of and support for citizens' assemblies. For many social movement activists, climate assemblies are a shorthand for a new way of doing democracy, one that challenges and disempowers entrenched interests that are resisting climate and ecological action. Their vision of climate assemblies is the empowerment of citizens to make decisions where governments fear to tread.

At the same time, public authorities are struggling with climate governance in a context, particularly in Europe, where many have committed to Net Zero. When many authorities declared a climate and ecological emergency, the continued pressure from social movements like XR and the youth-led Fridays for Future raised the profile of climate assemblies as a policy option. So too did the success of the Irish in dealing with abortion. Elected and appointed officials had evidence that assemblies could work and saw them as the 'next big thing'. And a small number of practitioner organisations with experience in running deliberative processes were available to work with public authorities to deliver assemblies. The stars were aligned.

But it is an odd movement. Most active in Europe are practitioners who design and deliver deliberative processes (not just on climate), activists associated with more radical climate movements, academics working on different aspects of deliberative democracy and a few public officials and politicians who have had direct experience of climate assemblies and found them transformational to their ways of working.

KNOCA has played a key role in bringing these different actors together, building the knowledge base and helping to shape future practice. KNOCA was established by the European Climate Foundation (ECF) in 2021. ECF's interest in assemblies comes from the top. Its CEO, Laurence Tubiana, was one of the co-Chairs of the Governance Committee of the French Citizens' Convention for the Climate and was convinced that we need a better understanding of the role that assemblies could play. A declaration of interest – I am the founding Chair of KNOCA!

KNOCA has over 700 individuals as part of its community. A decision was made not to have institutional membership given the challenges of holding the ring that includes both national governments and XR. The shared interest of the KNOCA community, wherever they are from, is to improve commissioning, design, implementation, evaluation and impact of assemblies. This is something that everyone can sign up to while having very different visions of future trajectories for climate assemblies.

Within the KNOCA community, relatively few are established actors within climate governance: elected politicians, civil servants and mainstream climate NGOs. Those who have or are about to commission and organise assemblies are active. But they have been converted to the cause through direct experience – or the need to know how to run an effective process.

As we discussed earlier in the book, we find scepticism and at times open hostility towards assemblies from those working within the existing institutions of climate governance.[20] One source of that disposition is professional status. Highly educated, technical experts often find it hard to believe that ordinary people can handle complex issues and are worried that assemblies are a delaying tactic when action is needed now. They tend to know little about how assemblies work and some believe that they will be open to capture by those trying to delay action and will make recommendations with low ambitions. Others are worried that they will be taken over and dominated by radical climate activists. Criticism is not consistent.

We've already discussed how direct experience of climate assemblies turned Chris Stark, the CEO of the Climate Change Committee in the UK and Eva Saldaña, Director of Greenpeace Spain, into advocates for deliberative processes. It is climate professionals like Stark and Saldaña who can cut through prevalent biases in a way that others cannot.

But Stark also highlights the challenge of navigating such a diverse movement. He contends that one of the reasons why Climate Assembly UK had so little influence is because of the protest activities of XR. Climate assemblies became too associated with the direct action movement, turning many parliamentarians and the government away from the assembly and its recommendations.

> There is a political aspect to this resistance. It was slightly undermined by campaign groups who were asking for a citizens' assembly with binding outputs. I make no real comment on that, except to say that some of the select committees were hesitant to work with the findings of Climate Assembly UK as a result.[21]

This is going to remain a tension. At times radical activism will open up spaces for climate assemblies. At other times, it will undermine government support. That's what happens in most movements for change.

Two new sets of actors could have a profound impact on the future of climate assemblies.

The first is the growing interest in assemblies amongst those working within arts and culture. Their impact could be both internal and external. Internal in the sense that they might develop creative practices that cultivate and strengthen imagination and collaborative working within assemblies. External in the sense that they will contribute to more creative and engaging communication of the potential of climate assemblies – not just effecting robust media strategies when a particular assembly is happening, but making citizens' assemblies part of our everyday public conversations. This requires cultural reproduction. One of the reasons why XR has been able to capture people's imagination is its use of striking imagery and iconography. The desire by leading visual and media artists, musicians, writers, comedians and others to centre citizens' assemblies within their work promises to take assemblies from their niche into more mainstream culture.[22]

A second powerful group of new advocates is previous assembly members. In many assemblies, little or no attention is given to supporting assembly members once the report has been agreed. In some, for example, Ireland, this is an explicit decision. Members have done their work. Now it is time for the professional politicians and civil servants to do theirs. Others have a more expansive idea of the role that assembly members could play – including many members themselves.[23]

We glimpsed one possible approach with Les 150 in France. Members formed their own civic association and played a key role in the public debate that followed the Convention. In Estonia, some of the members of the Ida-Viru youth assembly went on to form a new civic organisation to raise climate awareness in the region which now sits on the steering committee of the Ministry of Finance's Just Transition Fund. Members of the Blackburn with

Darwen People's Jury on the Climate Crisis in the UK worked together not only to monitor the local authority, but also to meet with their local MPs and work with local artists to raise awareness of their recommendations. In Denmark, the Høsholm Climate Citizens' Panel was offered training in community organising with the aim of strengthening their capacity for climate action.

Precisely what the social and political roles for members might be post-assembly is still very much an open question. No doubt different members will be up for different types of activities, whether it be holding public officials and stakeholders to account, speaking at public events and demonstrations or community organising and development. What we do know already is that members' authentic voices can cut through in a way that is different to and often much more effective than seasoned policy professionals, elected politicians, activists or academics. They have a qualitatively different experience to share that is grounded in their everydayness. The power of democratic lottery and deliberation can be the basis not only for the emergence of a new form of participatory climate governance, but also a new type of climate actor. Our understanding of how we build the civic infrastructure to support, develop and sustain the capacity of members is only in its infancy – and will need to be a process of co-creation with members themselves.

The movement for climate assemblies is still in its early stages but already an impressive array of organisations and individuals are active in commissioning, delivering, evaluating and advocating for assemblies. The conversations around assemblies are more sophisticated and grounded. Alternative futures are being articulated and acted on. Differences in goals and strategy are to be expected within a fertile movement. This diversity should be celebrated.

CHAPTER 5

Concluding Thoughts

If I had been told five years ago that we would have this much activity around climate assemblies, I would not have believed it. It is quite remarkable how much energy and creativity has been put into assemblies, not least from the diverse groups of citizens who have shared their collective wisdom on how to confront the climate and ecological crisis.

We can draw at least three lessons from all this activity.

First, citizens' assemblies show us that another way of doing climate politics is possible. The combination of democratic lottery and deliberation creates a hopeful, generative, human space in which the common sense of citizens can be brought to bear on the pressing challenges we face. We can work together constructively to build a different future.

Second, we are in a much better place to understand how to organise assemblies in ways that enable and sustain their impact.

Third, we need to be realistic about what assemblies can achieve. We can be confident that within well-designed assemblies, citizens come to robust judgements on the dilemmas we face. Where more considered work is needed is figuring out the ways that assemblies can be embedded within our political systems, whether this is assemblies organised by governments and other public bodies or by civil society organisations and social movements. Assemblies can be embedded to supplement existing liberal representative institutions in developing stronger climate policy or as independent bodies that challenge established powerholders to take action. Either way, we need to better understand how assemblies relate to other institutions, organisations and movements.

We are in danger of expecting too little and too much of climate assemblies. Both will end in disappointment.

Expect too little and climate assemblies will disappoint as organisers shy away from asking citizens to consider political and social dilemmas with material consequences on our lives. Expect too little and our fellow citizens will not feel trusted enough to do the necessary work. We will lose a way of opening up new possibilities for climate action. We will fall back on tried and tested forms of climate governance that have simply not worked – and will continue to fail us.

This would represent a massive failure of political imagination.

Expect too much and climate assemblies will disappoint because they cannot alone deliver the transformative changes that are necessary. To just organise citizens' assemblies and assume that their recommendations will be enough to shift a dysfunctional political system is misguided.

This too would represent a massive failure of political imagination.

We can steer a different path. This does not mean that we forgo imagination and creativity. They will be essential if a new democratic climate politics is to emerge and be sustained.

We need to think about assemblies in relation to an unfolding crisis. The climate and ecological crisis cannot be solved once and for all. We will live together on a warming planet and humans and nonhuman nature will have to adapt. We need to renew our democratic systems to help us navigate the emerging demands in ways that ensure climate and ecological justice.

Climate assemblies can – and I would argue, should – be part of that system renewal. We need to figure out how assemblies can best be embedded with other parts of the political system that themselves may need to be reformed and restructured. In this book, I've shown how some of that work is underway, in terms of the relationship with public bodies and civil society organisations that commission assemblies and emerging practices of stakeholder and broader public engagement.

This is only the beginning of the work that is necessary.

We need to combine this imaginative, creative work with a more hard-headed analysis of political power and how to enact change through assemblies. We need to find ways of working together to confront entrenched interests in our societies that are hostile to the democratic renewal of climate governance.

The last five years have shown that we can create inspiring, diverse democratic spaces that generate public wisdom on pressing climate and ecological challenges. The next five years require us to build the broader social and political conditions in which climate assemblies thrive and help effect meaningful and transformative change. So, let's get to work!

Endnotes

Acknowledgements

[1] https://knoca.eu/

Introduction

[1] The assembly website explains the details of the Convention and its report https://www.conventioncitoyennepourleclimat.fr/en/. A short summary of the Convention and other national assemblies can be found at https://www.knoca.eu/climate-assemblies#Summaries-of-national-climate-assemblies

[2] Collectif, *La Grande Désillusion: Vécus de la Convention Citoyenne sur le Climat*. France: Atlande, 2023.

[3] https://factuel.afp.com/doc.afp.com.32JD6RY

[4] Mathieu Saujot, Nicolas Berghmans, Andreas Ruedinger, Sébastien Treyer, Michel Colombier, Laura Brimont and Yann

Briand, *The Citizens' Climate Convention: 149 Measures for a New Vision of the Transition*. Study No. 7. Paris: IDDRI, 2020. https://www.iddri.org/sites/default/files/PDF/Publications /Catalogue%20Iddri/Etude/ST0720-CCC%20EN.pdf

[5] https://globalassembly.org/

[6] The Paris Agreement is a legally binding international treaty which commits nations to ensure that the increase in global average temperature stays well below two degrees Celsius above pre-industrial levels, with an ambition to stay below 1.5 degrees. See https://unfccc.int/process-and-meetings/the -paris-agreement

[7] https://www.assembleeclimat.brussels/lassemblee/

[8] https://medium.com/participo/2023-trends-in-deliberative -democracy-oecd-database-update-c8802935f116

Chapter 1: Why Climate Assemblies?

[1] The analysis of drivers of short-termism are elaborated in Graham Smith, *Can Democracy Safeguard the Future?* Cambridge: Polity, 2021.

[2] G. Supran, S. Rahmstorf and N. Oreskes, 'Assessing Exxon-Mobil's Global Warming Projections', *Science*, 379(6628). https://doi.org/10.1126/science.abk0063

[3] Martin Rees, 'If I Ruled the World'. *Prospect*, 21 August 2014. http://www.prospectmagazine.co.uk/regulars/if-i-ruled-the -world-martin-rees

[4] European Commission, *The European Green Deal*. COM/ 2019/640 final, p. 22. https://eur-lex.europa.eu/legal-content /EN/TXT/?uri=COM%3A2019%3A640%3AFIN

[5] Hélène Landemore, *Democratic Reason: Politics, Collective Intelligence and the Rule of the Many*. Princeton: Princeton University Press, 2013.

[6] Maija Setälä and Graham Smith, 'Mini-Publics and Deliberative Democracy'. In *The Oxford Handbook of Deliberative*

Democracy, edited by André Bächtiger, John S. Dryzek, Jane J. Mansbridge and Mark E. Warren. Oxford: Oxford University Press, 2018. pp. 300–314.

7 http://climateandenergy.wwviews.org/

8 For references and links to these examples, see Smith, *Can Democracy Safeguard the Future?* pp. 94–95.

9 Graham Smith, Tim Hughes, Lizzie Adams and Charlotte Obijiaku (eds.), *Democracy in a Pandemic: Participation in Response to Crisis*. London: University of Westminster Press, 2021. https://www.uwestminsterpress.co.uk/site/books/e/10.16997/book57/

10 For more on the Greek use of sortition and its broader historical and contemporary impact, see Yves Sintomer, *The Government of Chance*. Cambridge: Cambridge University Press, 2023.

11 Irene Alonso Toucido and Yves Dejaeghere,'Organising a Democratic Lottery'. Belgium: Federation for Innovation in Democracy – Europe, 2022. https://static1.squarespace.com/static/5fe06832bfc2b9122d70c45b/t/63811fa466ef155fd6bf6acf/1669406633663/FIDE+-+Organising+a+Democratic+Lottery.pdf; MASS LBP, 'How to Run a Civic Lottery: Designing Fair Selection Mechanisms for Deliberative Public Processes, A Guide and License, Version 1.4'. Toronto: MASS LBP, 2017. https://static1.squarespace.com/static/6005ceb747a6a51d636af58d/t/6010cf8f038cf00c5a546bd7/1611714451073/civiclotteryguide.pdf

12 https://www.hallobundestag.de/en/the-project-hallo-bundestag/outreach-random-selection-method

13 André Bächtiger, John S. Dryzek, Jane J. Mansbridge and Mark E. Warren (eds.), *The Oxford Handbook of Deliberative Democracy*. Oxford: Oxford University Press, 2018.

14 Claus Offe and Ulrich K. Preuss, 'Democractic Institutions and Moral Resources'. In *Political Theory Today*, edited by David Held. Standford. Standford University Press. 1991.

15 Daniel Kahneman,*Thinking, Fast and Slow. London: Penguin, 2011.*

Chapter 2: Learning From the First Wave

[1] For summaries of completed national assemblies, see https://www.knoca.eu/climate-assemblies#Summaries-of-national-climate-assemblies

[2] For an analysis of climate assemblies beyond Europe, see Nicole Curato, Graham Smith and Rebecca. Willis, *Deliberative Democracy and Climate Change: Exploring the Potential of Climate Assemblies in the Global South*. Stockholm: International IDEA, 2024. https://doi.org/10.31752/idea.2024.34

[3] For a useful schematic of the different phases of a citizens' assembly see https://assemblyguide.demnext.org/

[4] John Boswell, Rikki Dean and Graham Smith, 'Integrating Citizen Deliberation into Climate Governance: Lessons on Robust Design from Six Climate Assemblies'. *Public Administration* 101, no. 1 (2023). https://doi.org/10.1111/padm.12883

[5] The details of many of these organisations can be found on the website of Democracy R&D https://democracyrd.org/about/

[6] Laurence Tubiana, CEO of the European Climate Foundation (ECF), was one of the co-chairs of the Convention. It is because of her direct experience in the process that ECF launched the Knowledge Network on Climate Assemblies (KNOCA).

[7] https://bluedemocracy.pl/

[8] Louis-Gaëtan Giraudet et al., '"Co-construction" in Deliberative Democracy: Lessons from the French Citizens' Convention for Climate'. *Humanities and Social Sciences Communications*, 9, no. 1 (2022). https://doi.org/10.1057/s41599-022-01212-6

[9] Saujot et al., *The Citizens' Climate Convention*.

[10] Jonas Lage, Johannes Thema, Carina Zell-Ziegler, Benjamin Best, Luisa Cordroch, Frauke Wiese, 'Citizens Call for Sufficiency and Regulation: A Comparison of European Citizen Assemblies and National Energy and Climate Plans', *Energy Research & Social Science*, 104 (2023): 103254. https://doi.org/10.1016/j.erss.2023.103254

[11] Climate Assembly UK, *The Path to Net Zero: Climate Assembly UK Full Report* (2020), p. 26. https://www.climateassembly.uk/recommendations/index.html

[12] Saujot et al., *The Citizens' Climate Convention*, pp. 11–12.

[13] Convention Citoyenne pour le Climate, *Citizens' Convention on Climate Report: Summary*. English version. (2020), pp. 6–7. https://www.conventioncitoyennepourleclimat.fr/wp-content /uploads/2020/07/062020-CCC-propositions-synthese-EN .pdf

[14] The Citizens' Assembly, *Report of the Citizens' Assembly on Biodiversity Loss* (2023), p. 16. https://citizensassembly.ie /reports/

[15] Scotland's Climate Assembly, *Recommendations for Action* (2021), p. 44. https://webarchive.nrscotland.gov.uk/202203211 33037/https://www.climateassembly.scot/

[16] This discussion of impact draws on the KNOCA Impact Evaluation Framework https://knoca.eu/impact-evaluation -framework/

[17] https://multinationales.org/en/investigations/who-s-after -the-french-citizens-climate-convention-171/

[18] Alina Averchenkova, Arnaud Koehl and Graham Smith, *KNOCA Briefing. Policy Impact of the French Citizens' Convention for the Climate: Untangling the Fate of the Citizens' Recommendations*. Brussels: KNOCA, 2024. https://www.knoca.eu /resources#briefings

[19] https://www.theccc.org.uk/2022/09/21/using-deliberative -policy-design-methods-to-support-better-climate-policy making/

[20] Jake Ainscough, 'Why Understanding What People Think is Crucial to the Next Phase of Climate Policy: Interview with Chris Stark', *Foundation for Democracy and Sustainable Development Newsletter*, Winter 2022. https://www.fdsd.org/2022 -interview-chris-stark/

[21] Lala Muradova, *KNOCA Briefing: Survey Experiments and Climate Assemblies*. Brussels: KNOCA, 2024. https://www.knoca .eu/resources#briefings

[22] Katrin Praprotnik, Daniela Ingruber, Sarah Nash, Roman Rodenko, *Evaluation Report of the Austrian 'Klimarat'. UWK, Assessment of the Perspectives of the Members and the Public*, University for Continuing Education Krems (UWK), 2022.

https://www.donau-uni.ac.at/dam/jcr:f8f52750-1594-485e
-9f4f-89efc0ad2d32/SACCA_final%20report_UWKpart.pdf

[23] Personal communication, 8 March 2024.

[24] https://extinctionrebellion.uk/2023/06/30/experiencing-a
-citizens-assembly-building-the-peoples-plan-for-nature/

[25] Sarah Allan, 'Climate Assembly Members Think and Act Differently on Climate, Two Years On', *Involve* (blog), 11 January 2023. https://involve.org.uk/news-opinion/projects/climate
-assembly-members-think-and-act-differently-climate-two
-years

Chapter 3: Enhancing Impact

[1] This section draws on Stephanie Brancaforte and Janosch Pfeffer, *KNOCA Briefing. Setting the Remit for a Climate Assembly: Key Questions for Commissioners*. Brussels: KNOCA, 2022. https://www.knoca.eu/guidances-documents/setting-the
-remit

[2] John Kingdon, *Agenda, Alternatives and Public Policies*. Boston: Little, Brown, 1984.

[3] I extend the idea of competing logics from Lukas Kübler, Giulia Molinengo and Monika Arzberger, 'Towards Collaborative Governance: Why Innovation in Deliberative Democracy and the Public Sector Must Go Hand in Hand'. *Foundation for Democracy and Sustainable Development* (blog), 12 December 2022. https://www.fdsd.org/collaborative-governance/

[4] Ainscough, 'Why Understanding What People Think is Crucial to the Next Phase of Climate Policy'.

[5] Alina Averchenkova and Mara Ghilan, *KNOCA Briefing. Attitudes of Climate Policy Actors Towards Climate Assemblies Briefing*. Brussels: KNOCA, 2023. https://www.knoca.eu
/briefings/attitudes-of-climate-policy-actors-towards-climate
-assemblies

[6] Pete Bryant and Morten Friis, *Post Climate Assembly and Jury Support and Action. KNOCA Guidance*. Brussels: KNOCA, 2024. https://knoca.eu/guidance/

7 Joan Font, Graham Smith, Carol Galais and Pau Alarcón, 'Cherry-Picking Participation: Explaining the Fate of Proposals from Participatory Processes', *European Journal of Political Research*. 57, no. 3 (2018). https://doi.org/10.1111/1475-6765.12248; Jose Luis Fernandez Martinez, Joan Font and Graham Smith, 'The Sin of Omission? The Public Justification of Cherry-Picking'. In *The Impacts of Democratic Innovations*, edited by Vincent Jacquet, Matt Ryan and Ramon van der Does. Colchester: ECPR Press, 2023, pp. 233–254.

8 https://citizensassembly.ie/citizens-assembly-on-biodiversity-loss/terms-of-reference/

9 Muradova, *Survey Experiments and Climate Assemblies.*

10 See the Special Issue of the *Journal of Deliberative Democracy*, 'Democracy without Shortcuts', 16 no. 2 (2020), on the work of Christina Lafont. https://delibdemjournal.org/issue/65/info/

11 https://www.odoxa.fr/sondage/mesures-de-convention-citoyenne-seduisent-francais-a-lexception-notable-110-km-h/

12 https://peoplesplanfornature.org/national-conversation

13 Sandover, Rebecca, Alice Moseley, and Patrick Devine-Wright. 'Contrasting views of citizens' assemblies: Stakeholder perceptions of public deliberation on climate change.' *Politics and Governance* 9. no.2 (2021): 76–86. https://www.cogitatiopress.com/politicsandgovernance/article/view/4019/2079

14 https://globalassembly.org/community-assemblies

15 https://www.noemamag.com/democracys-missing-link/

Chapter 4: Where Next for Climate Assemblies?

1 Ernesto Ganuza and Gianpaolo Baiocchi, 'The Power of Ambiguity: How Participatory Budgeting Travels the Globe', *Journal of Deliberative Democracy*, 8 no. 2 (2012). https://doi.org/10.16997/jdd.142

2 This section builds on Nabila Abbas, *KNOCA Briefing. Towards Permanent Climate Citizens' Assemblies*. Brussels: KNOCA, 2024. https://www.knoca.eu/resources#briefings

3 Teresa R. Melgar, 'A Time of Closure? Participatory Budgeting in Porto Alegre, Brazil, After the Workers' Party Era'. *Journal of Latin American Studies*, 46, no.1 (2014). https://doi.org/10.1017/S0022216X13001582; Rikki Dean, John Boswell and Graham Smith, 'Designing Democratic Innovations as Deliberative Systems: The Ambitious Case of NHS Citizen'. *Political Studies*, 68, no. 3 (2020). https://doi.org/10.1177/0032321719866002

4 KNOCA Workshop on Citizens' Assemblies Commissioned by Civil Society, 10 April 2024. https://www.knoca.eu/events/workshop-on-climate-assemblies-commissioned-by-civil-society

5 https://www.knoca.eu/national-assemblies/polish-citizens-assembly-on-energy-poverty

6 https://wp.unil.ch/assemblee-transition/assemblee/

7 https://rogerhallam.com/citizens-assemblies-from-pr-fodder-of-the-carbon-state-to-revolutionary-confrontation-with-the-carbon-state/

8 Intergovernmental on Climate Change, *Special Report: Global Warming of 1.5°C*. Cambridge: Cambridge University Press, 2018. https://doi.org/10.1017/9781009157940

9 Intergovernmental Science-Policy Platform on Biodiversity and Ecosystem Services, *Global Assessment Report on Biodiversity and Ecosystem Services*. Bonn: IPBES, 2019. https://doi.org/10.5281/zenodo.3831673

10 Saujot et al., *The Citizens' Climate Convention*, p. 1.

11 Claire Mellier and Stuart Capstick, *How Can Citizens' Assemblies Help Navigate the Systemic Transformations Required by the Polycrisis? Learnings and Recommendations for Practitioners, Policymakers, Researchers, and Civil Society*. Bath: CAST guidelines, 2024. https://cast.ac.uk/

12 David Kahane, 'Climate Change, Social Change and System Change'. In *Public Deliberation on Climate Change: Lessons from Alberta Climate Dialogue*, edited by Lorelei I. Hanson. Edmonton: Athabasca University Press, 2018. https://www.aupress.ca/app/uploads/120271_99Z_Hanson_2018-Public_Deliberation_on_Climate_Change.pdf

[13] Nicole Curato et al., *Global Assembly on the Climate and Ecological Crisis Evaluation Report*. Canberra: University of Canberra, 2023. https://researchprofiles.canberra.edu.au/en /publications/global-assembly-on-the-climate-and-ecological -crisis-evaluation-r

[14] https://www.youtube.com/playlist?list=PL2MU0IRbuXDO vu0-InIrkOTNk9SeUseoX

[15] KNOCA Workshop on Systems Thinking in Climate Assemblies, 1 Feb 2024. https://www.knoca.eu/events/workshop-on -systems-thinking-in-climate-assemblies

[16] Mellier and Capstick, *How Can Citizens' Assemblies Help Navigate the Systemic Transformations Required by the Polycrisis?*; See also David Kahane, *Thinking Systemically About Deliberative Democracy and Climate Change*. London, Foundation for Democracy and Sustainable Development, 2016. http://www .fdsd.org/wp-content/uploads/2016/01/Deliberative-demo cracy-and-climate-change-Kahane.pdf

[17] Katie Reid, *Children and Young People's Participation in Climate Assemblies: KNOCA Guidance Document*. Brussels: KNOCA, 2024. https://www.knoca.eu/guidances-documents /children-and-young-peoples-participation-in-climate -assemblies

[18] KNOCA Workshop, 'Hearing Unheard Voices: Listening to Future and Generations and Nonhuman Nature in Climate Assemblies, 17 January 2024. https://www.knoca.eu/events /workshop-on-hearing-unheard-voices

[19] https://extinctionrebellion.uk/decide-together/

[20] Averchenkova and Ghilan, *KNOCA Briefing. Attitudes of Climate Policy Actors Towards Climate Assemblies.*

[21] Ainscough, 'Why Understanding What People Think is Crucial to the Next Phase of Climate Policy'.

[22] In the UK, the Hard Art collective has shown a particular interest in citizens' assemblies. See https://hardart.metalabel.com/

[23] Bryant and Friis, *Post-Climate Assembly and Jury Member Support and Action.*

About the Author

Graham Smith is Professor of Politics at the Centre for the Study of Democracy, University of Westminster, UK. He is a globally recognised expert on democratic innovations – new forms of public participation in political decision making. His book *Democratic Innovations: Designing Institutions for Citizen Participation* (Cambridge University Press, 2009) helped define this field of study.

In 2021 he was appointed the founding Chair of the Knowledge Network on Climate Assemblies (KNOCA), funded by the European Climate Foundation. This role builds on his international reputation for collaborating with governments, practitioners, civil society organisations and activists to build robust climate and democratic governance. He has been recognised by Apolitical as one of the Top 100 Most Influential Academics in Government.

Recent publications include *Can Democracy Safeguard the Future?* (Polity, 2021) and *Democracy in a Pandemic: Participation in Response to Crisis* (University of Westminster Press, 2021), edited with colleagues at the participation charity Involve.

Until recently he was Chair of the Foundation for Democracy and Sustainable Development and is a long-time collaborator with Participedia and Democracy R&D.

Index